ADVANCE PRAISE FOR *BREWED IN MICHIGAN*

"*Brewed in Michigan* is certainly the most comprehensive study yet of the crucible that is Michigan craft brewing. Bill Rapai's book incisively captures the collaborative passion and philosophy we brewers share, as well as the diversity of our no-longer-fledgling craft beer movement. He lends real insight into the big question: 'Why Michigan beer?'"

—Ted Badgerow, founder of The Real Ale Company and head brewer/owner of the Ypsi Alehouse

"Kudos to Mr. Rapai for capturing the history and individual stories of the craft beer industry in Michigan. Equally impressive is his recognition of the important but lesser-known pioneers like Ben Edwards and Tom Burns."

—John Linardos, founder of Motor City Brewing Works

"*Brewed in Michigan* is an outstanding example of all the good that comes from beer. Beyond the tours of breweries selected from around the state and the entrepreneurial personalities behind them is a story of industry rebirth and community redevelopment. Beer enthusiasts throughout Michigan and beyond will enjoy this quick, easy read about Michigan's newest and most successful industry. This is a pure Michigan story that will also be of great interest to researchers, community leaders, and politicians wishing to tap into what makes Michigan the great beer state."

—Rex Halfpenny, publisher of *Michigan Beer Guide*

BREWED IN MICHIGAN

BREWED IN MICHIGAN

The New Golden Age of Brewing in the Great Beer State

WILLIAM RAPAI

A Painted Turtle book

ISBN 978-0-8143-4210-7 (paperback)
ISBN 978-0-8143-4211-4 (ebook)

Library of Congress Cataloging Number: 2017939700

Painted Turtle is an imprint of Wayne State University Press

Wayne State University Press
Leonard N. Simons Building
4809 Woodward Avenue
Detroit, Michigan 48201-1309

Visit us online at wsupress.wayne.edu

FOR THE LOVELY JOANN

WANNA GET A BEER TONIGHT?

CONTENTS

Acknowledgments ix

Life After Stroh's 1

If Beer Is Beer, What's Different? 11

1. AN INDUSTRY REBORN 29

Bell's Brewery / Kalamazoo

Motor City Brewing Works / Detroit

Arbor Brewing Company / Ann Arbor, Ypsilanti, Bengaluru (Karnataka, India)

2. A LIQUID CANVAS 51

Short's Brewing Company / Bellaire

Right Brain Brewery / Traverse City

Jolly Pumpkin Artisan Ales / Dexter, Ann Arbor, Detroit, Traverse City, Royal Oak

Schramm's Mead / Ferndale

Psycho Brew / Greenville

3. COOL PLACES 85

Pigeon Hill Brewing Company / Muskegon

Brite Eyes Brewing Company / Kalamazoo

Tahquamenon Falls Brewery & Pub / Paradise

The Old Mill Brewpub & Grill / Plainwell

Salt Springs Brewery / Saline

Elk Street Brewery and Taproom / Sandusky

Ore Dock Brewing Company / Marquette

Redwood Steakhouse and Brewery / Flint

4. COLLABEERATION 117

Dark Horse Brewing Company / Marshall

Kuhnhenn Brewing Company / Warren, Clinton Township

Grizzly Peak Brewing Company / Ann Arbor

It's Women's Work

Brewery Vivant / Grand Rapids

5. BEER MAKES THE WORLD GO 'ROUND 145

Cedar Springs Brewing Company / Cedar Springs

Batch Brewing Company / Detroit

Fort Street Brewery / Lincoln Park

6. BEER BRINGS PEOPLE TOGETHER FOR THE BETTER 161

Atwater Brewery / Detroit, Grand Rapids, Grosse Pointe Park

Greenbush Brewing Company / Sawyer

Royal Oak Brewery / Royal Oak

Stormcloud Brewing Company / Frankfort

Founders Brewing Company / Grand Rapids

Cheboygan Brewing Company / Cheboygan

Dragonmead Microbrewery / Warren

Detroit Beer Company / Detroit

Frankenmuth Brewery / Frankenmuth

Saugatuck Brewing Company / Douglas

Last Call 205

Notes 209

Index 211

ACKNOWLEDGMENTS

The inspiration for this book comes from my youngest brother Steve, who is more commonly known as Munchkin. Munchkin is a guy who would happily crawl from Plymouth to Grand Rapids just to have a Backwoods Bastard in the Founders taproom.

A few years ago, I traveled extensively throughout Michigan while researching a book on invasive species in the Great Lakes. I like beer, and everywhere I went I made a point of stopping by the local brewery for a glass, viewing it as an opportunity to torment Munchkin. I would take a photo of the beer and send it to him by text.

Hey, it's what brothers do.

But one day shortly after completing the invasive species book, I got a surprising reply from Munchkin. Instead of the usual angry eye roll expressed in words, he sent a suggestion: "Your next book should be on Michigan beer."

Little did I know that, at the same time, Wayne State University Press was looking for an author to write a book about Michigan beer that would be a rough sequel to *Brewed in Detroit,* a history of brewing in southeastern Michigan written by former Stroh Brewing Company executive Peter H. Blum.

Kismet. Thank you, Munchkin! I guess I owe you more than a photo of a beer.

In the eighteen months I spent researching this book, I met a lot of people who were willing to share their knowledge and thoughts about why Michigan makes great beer. Two of them are Rex Halfpenny and Bill Wamby. They helped me understand the finer points of beer and always let me know in no uncertain terms if I was wandering off in the wrong direction. A special thank-you also goes to Jack Archiable, the "brewstorian" and jack-of-all-trades at Short's Brewing Company for sharing his sense of humor, knowledge, and perspective.

Thank you also to Kathy Wildfong and the staff at Wayne State University Press for their enthusiastic support for this project.

Thanks, of course, to Maggie and Julia for putting up with their dad's dinnertime beer stories even though they were underage. Ladies, if you take anything from your father's adventure, I hope you have learned that beer and other forms of alcohol are to be treated with respect.

Of course, the biggest thank-you goes to The Lovely Joann, who has now allowed me to write three books. Each project has given me great satisfaction—even if it did not necessarily enrich the family bank account. Joann, everything good in this book is because of you.

Finally, an extra special thank-you to my liver. For eighteen months I have abused you, and yet you continued to come to work every day and never once complained. I'm so proud of you!

LIFE AFTER STROH'S

BEER.

It's a simple four-letter word, and yet it's so evocative, so powerful, so magnetic. Consider what some of the greatest thinkers of all time have said about beer:

For many, beer is a passion. We go out of our way to find high-quality brands or experiment with unfamiliar styles. We think about it, discuss its qualities, study it as if we are researching a dissertation, and generally obsess over it. But why? Why should we invest so much of ourselves into a beverage?

Well, for starters, beer makes us feel good. The simple act of touching a glass of beer to our lips releases endorphins—chemicals that produce feelings of pleasure in our brains. When consumed in moderation, beer is a healthy drink. It contains antioxidants that are good for our bodies. It contains large amounts of vitamin B, and because it contains polyphenols, as red wine does, it even helps to lower our risk of heart disease.

Probably most of all, we love beer because it's a social beverage. We associate it with good times. We drink it when we are having fun with friends or even just chatting with a stranger at the bar. We drink it at the ballpark on a sunny day, celebrate a special occasion with it, and even court a potential mate with it.

Beer, it seems, nourishes us both physically and spiritually.

No beverage—other than water, obviously—has done more for Michigan than beer. Every ingredient that goes into beer—water, grain, hops, and yeast—is produced in Michigan. Coffee may power a state of hard-working people, but coffee is not produced here. And beer doesn't make us jittery.

> "HE WAS A WISE MAN WHO INVENTED BEER."
> —PLATO

> "WHOEVER DRINKS BEER, HE IS QUICK TO SLEEP; WHOEVER SLEEPS LONG, DOES NOT SIN; WHOEVER DOES NOT SIN, ENTERS HEAVEN! THUS, LET US DRINK BEER!"
> —MARTIN LUTHER

> "BEER. IT'S THE BEST DAMN DRINK IN THE WORLD."
> —JACK NICHOLSON

> "I WOULD KILL EVERYONE IN THIS ROOM FOR A DROP OF SWEET BEER."
> —HOMER SIMPSON

Cardboard boxes are stacked in one corner of the brewhouse at Griffin Claw in Birmingham, waiting to be filled with cans to be shipped to the distributor.

Larry Bell, the founder of Bell's Brewery in Kalamazoo, is considered by many the person who set the direction and provided inspiration for Michigan's craft brewing industry.

Of course, Michigan is not the only state that has beer. But Michigan is the only state that has *Michigan* beer. Michigan beer doesn't have its own style, but there certainly is a Michigan beer *pride* that separates us from every other midwestern state.

Initially that pride grew out of Detroit, the home of the Stroh Brewery, which was at one time the third-largest brewery in the United States. But that pride took a major hit on Friday, May 31, 1985, when Stroh management closed its flagship brewery and 135 years of tradition came to an end. Even people who believed Stroh's was only a step above unfiltered Detroit River water shed a tear at the news.

For most of the twentieth century, Stroh's was the biggest brewery in Michigan, and its 1-million-square-foot brewery on Gratiot Avenue on the eastern edge of downtown was a landmark in Detroit—its friendly red neon **STROH'S BEER** sign on the top of the brewhouse greeted drivers coming into city at the start of a workday and **S'HORTS REEB** shone in their rearview mirrors on their way home.

The closing of Stroh's Detroit brewery seemed to be just one more nail in the coffin for manufacturing in Michigan. Steel mills and auto plants were closing, and autoworkers were rapidly being replaced by robots and automation. In the Grand Rapids area, many furniture factories that drove western Michigan's economy had closed or were closing. The decline of manufacturing led many Michigan residents to pick up roots and flee for new opportunities in the Sunbelt.

But the same year that Stroh's closed in Detroit, a new model for the brewing industry was being born. In Kalamazoo, a young man named Larry Bell, a home brewer and owner of a brewing supply store, decided the time was right to open his own brewery. It would take nearly fifteen years for Bell's brewery to flourish, but he would become the Obi Wan Kenobi of Michigan brewing.

While Bell is regarded as a rock star hero in brewery circles today, Ben Edwards, practically unknown and largely forgotten, is arguably a more important figure in seeding Michigan's craft beer boom. In the mid-1980s, Edwards was a Detroit restaurateur and an early pioneer in the farm-to-table movement who longed to offer freshly brewed beer to his customers to complement his fresh-made breads

Fermentation vessels at Short's Brewing Company's production brewery in Elk Rapids.

and cheeses. When Edwards was not granted a brewer's license by the state, he led the effort to change Michigan's laws to allow for the creation of brewpubs.

Together, Bell and Edwards would usher in a new golden age of brewing in Michigan.

In the wake of Stroh's closing, high-quality breweries have popped up all over Michigan, and the state is now home to some of the most respected breweries in the country. Among them are:

- Bell's Brewery, which is now the oldest continually operating brewery in the state. Although Larry Bell teetered on the edge of bankruptcy twice and was pressured by investors to change his brewing style to make beers that were more widely appealing, he stuck to his philosophy: make good beer.

- Founders Brewery in Grand Rapids. Like Bell's, Founders draws beer tourists from all over the country to the taproom,

Atwater in the Park, in Grosse Pointe Park, occupies a building that was once Grace United Church of Christ.

particularly when the brewery releases one of its highly desired limited release brews like KBS.

- Short's Brewing in Bellaire, which has put a tiny Antrim County town on the national map. Short's has become a national leader in creative brewing, raking in awards for experimental beer at the Great American Beer Festival.

- Jolly Pumpkin Artisan Ales in Dexter, which was the first brewery in the country to bring an old Franco-Belgian brewing tradition to the United States and age all its beers in oak barrels. Brewer Ron Jeffries is viewed among his peers as a mensch for demanding that the beer be aged for as long as two years before bottling.

But there's more to the story than awards and respect. The brewing industry has been instrumental in helping to revive the economic fortunes of neighborhoods, towns, and entire cities. In 2014, brewing contributed more than $1.8 billion annually to Michigan's economy, according to an economic impact report from the Brewers Association, a trade association for craft brewers.[1] In 2015, Michigan ranked sixth in the number of craft breweries in the nation, and tenth in craft beer production.

Perhaps more important to beer lovers, the experience of visiting Michigan's breweries is second to none. Breweries occupy old churches, onetime auto dealerships, rehabilitated retail spaces, and converted restaurants. They're in big cities, tony suburbs, and farm towns. There's even one place you can go to make your own beer in addition to drinking it.

Brewers themselves have developed an ethic of camaraderie, collegiality, and cooperation. The struggle to make and sell a quality product in the 1990s—before craft beer caught on—brought brewers together to face tough economic challenges as they worked to educate people that there is more to life than fizzy

Ron Jeffries of Jolly Pumpkin in the brewery's Dexter Taproom.

yellow beer. That ethic of cooperation first and competition second is somewhat common among brewers nationwide, but in Michigan, it seems the bond among brewers is just a little stronger.

Craft beer, of course, is still beer, and it's made with the same ingredients that went into Stroh's, but this new generation of Michigan's brewers sees those ingredients as only a starting point. Beer today can be made with blueberries, pumpkins, asparagus, coffee, spices, and a myriad of other ingredients. These brewers see their work not as a job but as a craft, and they are reviving traditions that began in the seventeenth century when Europeans made beer on an artisanal scale. Those European brewing traditions came to North America first with English and Scottish immigrants, then with the Irish, Germans, and Slavs. Some brewers are staying true to the old traditions, while others are giving those traditions a twist.

While I was researching this book, brewer after brewer told me two things that they cherish about their craft: they love what they do because they work in an industry where they never stop learning, and they are attracted to beer in a quest for knowledge and novelty. They appreciate gaining a better understanding of the history of beer and its different styles; learning more about the ingredients that go into beer has deepened their appreciation for what they produce. At the same time, they still get excited when they encounter or create something new and unusual.

Although brewers have driven many of the changes in the Michigan beer scene, consumers have caught up and are now having considerable impact. Drinkers—particularly young drinkers—have shifted away from their father's lagers and have embraced more creative ales. Millennials are exerting their influence on the food culture in general by demanding locally made high-quality products, rejecting relatively inexpensive mass-produced items. Some young people proudly brag that they have never consumed a Bud Light.

The combination of those cultural shifts has made craft brewing a powerful movement that has in turn spurred other trends. As Michigan's beer enthusiasts demand locally made beers, Michigan brewers increasingly seek local ingredients. That has led to a renaissance in Michigan barley farming as well as malting and hops farming and processing.

But more than anything else, Michigan is the Great Beer State because of the individuals who are motivated by a passion for excellence and creativity. Michigan's brewers and beer drinkers have created a new culture, one that values quality over quantity, individuality within a community, and equal parts tradition and innovation. In a state that has been economically beaten and battered for forty years, brewing gives Michigan a new identity and restores our reputation as a place where products are thoughtfully engineered and carefully constructed. Beer—like the automobile—is now a part of the soul of this state.

Look at the top states in craft beer production and notice that five of them—California, Oregon, Colorado, North Carolina, and Michigan—share common characteristics: amazing natural resources and outdoor experiences, a rich agricultural heritage, creative and hardworking people, and a culture of innovation. But there's a difference between Michigan and those other states, and that's our spirit and our pride. That spirit is what makes Michigan the Great Beer State today and into the future.

⇒⟫⟫⟫⟩⟩─

This book owes an acknowledgment to Peter Blum, the former Stroh Brewery executive and author of *Brewed in Detroit: Breweries and Beer since 1830*. Blum's book, published by Wayne State University Press in 1998, is an outstanding history of brewing in Detroit and Michigan through the last decade of the twentieth century. Many brewers in the state told me they have read Blum's book—sometimes more than once—for its insight into the state's rich brewing tradition. But in the two decades since Blum's book appeared, the entire landscape of Michigan brewing has changed. In 1998, the state had only a handful of microbreweries, and the craft beer industry that dominates Michigan beer today was in its infancy. It is safe to say that Blum had no idea how much the craft brewing industry would grow and prosper.

That said, brewing is an industry that has always been in flux. Brewers have come and gone, and beer styles have risen and declined in popularity. The one constant is *passion*. Brewers are passionate about beer. They take what they do very seriously and come to work with one goal in mind: to make the today's beer better than yesterday's.

Even other brewers are eying Michigan with a mix of wonder and envy. In his keynote address to the Michigan Brewers Guild's annual winter conference in January 2017, Jim Koch, the co-founder and chairman of the company that brews the Boston-based Samuel Adams brands, said, referring to Michigan: "This is the best time, and the best place in the history of the world, to be a beer drinker. One hundred years from now, brewers will look back and say, 'I wish I could have been a part of this group.'"[2]

That passion has helped to burnish Michigan's image in the eyes of the nation. In 2014, Thrillist.com ranked Michigan as the fourth best beer state. The Beer Advocate website names Founders' CBS Imperial Stout the fifth best beer in the world and KBS (previously known as Kentucky Breakfast Stout) the fifteenth best. In fact, KBS has such a cult following that Founders and other businesses in Grand Rapids devote an entire week to the release of this limited edition brew every March, and beer tourists from around the country flock to the city to raise a pint.

So the goal of this book—forgive the pun—is to tap into Michigan's passion for beer. It is not a guide to Michigan's breweries; the brewing scene is changing so quickly that any book would be obsolete upon publication. Therefore, it also made no sense to attempt to visit every single brewery in the state. And I apologize in advance if you feel I overlooked your favorite breweries. At the start of the project, I made a list of breweries I thought it was important to write about. Some that I wanted to feature did not reciprocate the interest. We will leave it at that.

This book has a wide-ranging brief. Yes, it explores a new generation of brewers that is setting Michigan apart, the dramatic changes that have occurred in the state's brewing community over the past two decades, and the history of Michigan's craft beer movement. *Brewed in Michigan* also looks at the ethos of cooperation and support that has developed among brewers, how beer is revitalizing neighborhoods and communities, and how

Tenacity Brewing Company in Flint.

brewers today have thrown away old recipe books and are breaking taboos and pushing style boundaries to create new, unusual, creative, and just plain crazy stuff.

The advent of brewery taprooms and brewpubs has caused a change in the drinking culture as well. Craft beer is responsible for building communities and bringing people together. Sit in a brewery taproom and look around. Compared to the corner bar, where it's always dark so you don't see the stains on the carpet, craft brewery taprooms are open, airy, and clean. On Saturday and Sunday afternoons, it's surprising how many families visit a brewery taproom for a meal. Even though the clientele shifts at night, taprooms aren't a place for the surly guy who wants to be alone at the bar or for the party boy looking to get trashed. Brewery taprooms and brewpubs are warm and welcoming places. Some have music. Some offer trivia nights. Some have board games. Taprooms have become places where people gather for conversation to talk about families, current events, ways to improve cities and neighborhoods, and raise money for charities. Beer is beer, but craft beer is something more—it's a conduit to conversation.

But before we explore this new universe of brewing, let's start by asking a simple question: if beer is beer, what do Michigan's brewers do today that makes their beer different and special?

The taproom of Blackrocks Brewery is in an old house in a funky neighborhood on the outskirts of downtown Marquette.

IF BEER IS BEER, WHAT'S DIFFERENT?

In its most basic form, beer is a fermented beverage made from four ingredients: water, grains, hops, and yeast.

For years, Stroh's, Miller, Anheuser-Busch, Coors, and most other brewers gave beer drinkers a limited choice—a golden-colored, easy-drinking lager, or a watered-down light version of the same. Sure, there were some hard-to-find exceptions—Stroh's made a pretty good dark beer and every spring Anheuser-Busch makes a bock for the Michelob label. Despite the color of those beers, though, they were still malty, German-inspired beers. For the most part, there was little variation, and the biggest difference between brands was largely in how they were packaged and marketed.

But Michigan's brewers today experiment with those same four ingredients—water, grains, hops, and yeast—to achieve infinite variations of flavors and aromas. Years ago, the brewers at Stroh's challenged themselves to make the product as consistent as possible day in, day out. Today, the challenge for a brewer is to make consistently good beer *and* use new techniques and recipes to make something different or better with each batch. Success depends upon a brewer's experience and knowledge of ingredients, but it also depends on the desire to put up with sweat and wet socks, hours working with boiling liquids and caustic chemicals, and dealing with an ongoing case of brewer's drip—the sinus condition brewers endure caused by constantly going back and forth between the heat of the brewery and the chill of the cellar.

So, here's a 100-level class on brewing that will help you understand how brewers perform their magic, and why small decisions have large impacts.

> BEWARE THE LOLLIPOP OF MEDIOCRITY. LICK IT ONCE AND YOU WILL SUCK FOREVER.
> —A SIGN IN THE BREWERY AT DRAGONMEAD

MALTED BARLEY AND HOPS AT BREW DETROIT.

Clipboards on the brewing equipment in the pub at New Holland Brewing. Keeping good records is critical to brewing good beer.

Matt Greff, co-owner of Arbor Brewing Company in Ann Arbor and the Corner Brewery in Ypsilanti.

Think of beer as a tree trunk that splits into two limbs—one is lager and the other is ale. Every beer is one of those two. (Mead we can think of as the pretty flower that grows at the base of the tree. It's fermented and made with—or without—hops, but the fermented ingredient is honey, not grains, and therefore mead is not a limb on the beer tree.)

The process of making beer today is pretty much the same as it was when the last batch was made at Stroh's Detroit brewery: mix barley malt and hot water to make mash, drain the liquid out of the mash into the brew kettle, add hops and boil to make wort, move the wort to a fermentation vessel and add yeast, wait a prescribed period of time, add carbonation, and—voilà!—you have beer.

But today's brewers have taken liberties with that process, adding thousands of variables. Some don't even have a recipe in hand when they start to brew; often all they have is an idea in mind. Ron Jeffries, the brewer at Jolly Pumpkin in Dexter, says he starts with an idea of how he wants a beer to look, smell, and taste and works backward from there. When brewers take this approach, their knowledge of ingredients—what goes well with what and in what proportions—becomes critically important.

The first step in making beer is to make mash, a mixture of hot water and barley malt. But that's not as simple as it sounds because water is sometimes more than just water. Michigan is blessed with great water for brewing, but it's not perfect. If a brewery uses tap water from a city system, it contains chlorine. Even if the brewer takes steps to remove the chlorine, there's likely some calcium or other elements remaining that could potentially affect the taste of the beer. If a brewer's water comes from an aquifer, it could contain calcium, sulfur, iron, or arsenic. Or the water's pH could be too acidic or alkaline for the style of beer the brewer wants to make.

So, before anything else happens, a good brewer treats the water to prepare it for the specific style that is being brewed. Matt Greff, who co-owns Arbor Brewing with his wife, Rene, says the first

The first step in making malt is to wet barley kernels so they germinate.

step at his brewery is to run the water through a reverse osmosis system to remove salts and other impurities. That may sound like a good thing, but reverse osmosis doesn't discriminate, removing good stuff along with the bad and leaving brewers with mineral-free water. So the next step for brewers is to tweak the water for the specific type of beer that's being made. For a malty beer like a lager or a stout, it might be necessary to add calcium carbonate to enhance the malt flavor. Adding calcium sulfate—gypsum—will mellow the bitterness of the hops. For a hoppy beer like pale ale, it's best to start with water that is slightly acidic. For a doppelbock or Scotch ale, the addition of sodium will help bring out the malt's sweetness. "Some brewers don't treat [water], but it can be the difference between good beer and great beer," concludes Professor Cordell DeMattei, the director of fermentation studies at Central Michigan University.

The next step is to add grain to the water. Brewers mostly use barley; it gives beer its color, some of its aroma and flavor, its foamy head and, after fermentation, its alcohol. It's possible to brew beer without hops but it's impossible to make beer without barley or some other grain. (Sorghum is a common replacement and is the base of most gluten-free beers. Other beers—like Space Rock from Short's Brewing Company—are made gluten free by adding Brewers Clarex, an enzyme that breaks gluten's chemical bonds into easily digestible epitopes.)

But before the barley gets close to a brewery, it has to be made into malt. Malt is made by adding water to barley to force germination. Germination causes enzymes inside the grain to become active. If the grain were out in a field someplace, those enzymes would help the germinating plant break down starches inside the grain into sugars that will give the plant energy to grow until it's big enough to begin photosynthesis. Those sugars are critically important to the brewing process because they will eventually be consumed by the yeast and converted into alcohol.

So now that we've germinated those grains and woken up those enzymes, we have to put them back to sleep to stop the enzymes from breaking the starches into sugars. The goal, after all, is to save

Malt is removed from a kiln that has dried the barley and caused the sugars to go into a state of suspended animation.

those sugars for the yeast. The best way to stop the process is to put the grain in a state of suspended animation by drying it in a kiln. Malting keeps the enzymes and sugars stable, allowing the malt to be stored for several months without losing any of its sugars and enzymes.

Malting is one of humanity's oldest agricultural practices, and the basics of the operation have changed little. Wendell Banks, who runs Michigan Malt in Shepherd, a small, old-fashioned operation, says, "If we put on the right dungarees, you would have no idea it's not 1540."

Banks has been malting since 1999; for a while he was the only maltster in the state. Banks's operation makes only base malts—the type of malt that is most broadly used in beer. Other brewers in Michigan and elsewhere provide specialty malts that are dried longer or even roasted to give them characteristics that increase the specific flavor and smell of a beer. The expanded use of these specialty malts has been among the biggest changes in brewing since Stroh's closed.

Choosing the correct malts is important, but determining the right ratio of malts—specialty malt to base malt—is even more important. Dark malts impart so much flavor that a little goes a long way.

There may be different styles of malt, but they all come from one of two types of barley: six-row and two-row. The terms refer to the number of rows of grain on the floret, which is name for all those little seedpods at the top of the stalk. Although six-row varieties tend to grow better in the relatively humid Great Lakes region, craft brewers (and German brewers) mostly prefer the two-row varieties because the grain contains less protein. The protein level in the harvested barley is important because high levels of protein make beer cloudy or hazy. High protein levels also lead to a phenomenon called "gushing"; high-protein

Barley, ready for harvest, on a farm near Buckley. Barley farming is expanding rapidly in the state because many Michigan brewers want to brew with locally grown raw materials.

beer gushes out of a newly opened bottle similar to the way champagne floods out of a bottle that has been thoroughly shaken. Needless to say, most people hate it when their beer gushes.

The big boys in American brewing—Anheuser-Busch InBev, Pabst, and Coors—prefer six-row barley because those varieties tend to work better for beers that are made with adjuncts, which is the name given to additional ingredients like corn and rice.

Barley is a crop that makes farmers lose sleep because it is the only seed crop that has to be delivered to market alive. That means the annual barley harvest is a race against time for any farmer because a heavy rain could cause the seeds to germinate before they leave the field. If that happens, the crop is no longer usable for beer. The only alternative is to sell the barley as a feed crop, and there's not much of a market for feed barley because corn prices are almost always lower. Given all the potential problems with barley, Michigan farmers for decades shied away from growing it. The boom in Michigan brewing has assured farmers that the expanded market makes growing barley worth the risks. According to Michigan State University's Extension Service, ten thousand acres of barley were harvested in Michigan in 2013. In the following four years, that acreage doubled, and new malting operations opened in Traverse City and Muskegon to meet demand. According to a July 2014 bulletin from the extension service, in 2013 craft brewers nationally accounted for only 7.8 percent of market share, yet they consumed more than 25 percent of the malt used for beer. If craft brewing's market share reaches 10 percent, it's estimated that craft brewers will likely be consuming 31 percent of all the malt used for brewing in the United States.[3] Craft brewers generally use more malt in their products because they are seeking higher levels of alcohol than old-school lagers.

》》》》》

After the brewer has treated the water and decided on the proportion of various malts, the next step is to make mash by letting the malt steep in hot water in a vessel called the mash tun. During this

Six-row barley is more popular with lager brewers because its relatively high level of proteins works better in beers that contain adjuncts like corn and rice.

Bill Knudson, a Michigan State University Extension Service agent, checks progress on different varieties of barley at an experimental plot south of Traverse City.

Hops are added to the liquid during the boil. Hops impart flavor and their antiseptic properties help keep beer from spoiling.

process, which can take anywhere from forty-five to ninety minutes, the hot water breaks the sugars out of the barley—and the brewer will check Twitter, stir the mash, check email, stir the mash, look at the help-wanted ads in the latest issue of *Brewing* magazine, stir the mash, make sure the hoses are clean, stir the mash, check the pumps, stir the mash, order more malt, and, um, stir the mash. Despite being overcome by a sense that the universe can be a very boring place, the brewer cannot afford to stray from this duty. The number one job at this point is to ensure the temperature of the mash is constant.

"People often ask me, 'What do you do?' And I'm like, 'I don't do anything.' I mash in and then I let it sit and let the enzymes do their work," says Duncan Williams, the brewer at Grizzly Peak in Ann Arbor. "I'm more of a facilitator than anything else." Of course, in production breweries like Bell's or Founders, this process is automated, so the brewer's job all too often becomes one of monitoring the computer screen of a system that checks the mash temperature hundreds of times a minute.

Once the water and barley are done doing their thing, the brewer drains the liquid from the mash tun into the brew kettle. This sugary liquid is called wort (pronounced *wert*), and is ready for the next step—the addition of hops.

There are more than one hundred varieties of hops, and each has its own special qualities. Some taste like wet grass. Others have a citrus-like smell and bitterness. Still others smell like a pine forest or spices. Some hops provide flavors that last a long time, while others diminish quickly. (Which is why Founders no longer bottles Red's Rye IPA; the flavor of the Amarillo hops diminished so quickly that the quality of the beer was not what brewers wanted it to be by the time it hit store shelves.) The brewer's secret is to understand which varieties of hops will be best for the end product, then add them in the correct proportions to blend flavors and smells.

Hops add bitterness to beer. Highly hopped beers, like Bell's

The flower of the hop vine is used in brewing. The flower contains lupulin and oleoresin, which contribute flavor to beer.

Hopslam, derive their bitterness from the alpha acids produced by lupulin glands in the plant's cones. Bitterness is measured in IBU's—international bitterness units. The higher the number, of course, the more bitter the beer. Stroh's was lightly hopped, which was typical for a lager that usually ranges between five and thirteen IBUs. Although there's a general rule of thumb that the IBU number equals higher bitterness on the tongue, IBUs can be misleading since humans cannot taste bitterness above one hundred bitterness units. If somebody hands you a beer that has 150 or more IBU's, go ahead and try it. It won't kill you.

There is another way that IBU number can be misleading. Put two beers side by side. One may have an IBU of thirty-five, the other sixty-five. But—surprise!—that beer with an IBU of thirty-five might taste more bitter. How can that be? Even though a spectrometer can still measure those sixty-five IBUs, a good brewer can hide bitterness by balancing it with malt.

It's believed that hops were first used in beer in the ninth century. Before that, people flavored their beer with spices and plants, including pines and spruces, dandelions, marigolds, and tree bark. Brewers quickly switched to hops when they recognized that the plant's antibacterial qualities helped to prevent beer from spoiling.

It also appears that hops had a role in the creation of India Pale Ale. There are several murky and conflicting accounts of the origin of IPA, but one story purports that the style was invented out of necessity because beer being shipped from England to British troops in colonial India would spoil on the long trip around the southern tip of Africa. The problem was solved when brewers added more hops during the late stages of fermentation. The additional hops protected the treasured beverage from spoilage in the unrefrigerated wooden kegs. At the same time, wild yeast in the wood caused the beer to undergo a secondary fermentation during the trip, raising the level of alcohol.

Demand for Michigan-grown hops is increasing from brewers all around the country as beer drinkers continue to shift away from lightly hopped lagers to more flavorful ales. How flavorful is this new generation of beer? Craft brewers may produce only 13 percent of the beer in the United States, but they consume 50 percent of the hops.

Alex Wiesen and his father, Dan, co-owners of Empire Hops Farm west of Traverse City, are scrambling to meet the demand. The Wiesens were the first large-scale hops farmers in the state. The two had been longtime apple farmers in the Leelanau Peninsula when, in 2008, Dan Weisen read about a pending hops shortage and saw an opportunity.

The decision to switch to hops was practically a no-brainer since the family had a piece of land that wasn't good for growing apples. The Wiesens started cautiously, though, planting just five acres of hops after multiple conversations with Traverse City–area brewers; those brewers made it clear that before they would buy their hops the Wiesens needed to prove that they could provide a consistent, high-quality product from year to year.

Susan McCabe, owner of Ribbon Hops Farm in Detroit, checks the progress of hops being grown on an experimental plot in southwest Detroit.

With the experience gained from those first couple of years, Empire Hops Farm now grows five varieties on one hundred acres, and Alex Wiesen spends much of his time consulting with new hops farms that are sprouting up all over the state. Wiesen believes that in less than a decade Michigan has equaled Pacific Northwest hops in quality and is quickly catching up in quantity and price.

Wiesen will be the first to tell you that hops are not easy to grow, partially because they prefer sandy soils. But one entrepreneur is trying to make a go of hops farming in the clay-rich soils of Detroit. The trend to urban farming is led by hip, young, socially aware entrepreneurs, but new hops farmer Susan McCabe, a retired museum docent, bucks the trend. An inveterate gardener, and home brewer, McCabe was inspired to start growing hops after a conversation with a Detroit brewer who was looking for a steady supply of hops from an urban farm. Seeing an opportunity, McCabe submitted a grant proposal to a competition sponsored by the Michigan Women's Foundation. The foundation liked what it heard and awarded McCabe $7,500 to start Ribbon Hops Farm.

Since committing to the effort, McCabe has faced two major challenges. The first is finding a Detroit location where the soil isn't contaminated from industry and doesn't contain lots of rubble. The second is building a trellis system that will maximize space in a cramped urban environment and allow for an easy harvest of twenty-foot-tall vines without a harvesting machine. She grows Fuggle, Hallertau, Glacier, Saaz, and Mackinac varieties, and so far she has sold her hops mostly to home brewers.

Depending on what's being made, the brewer at this point will go ahead with a simple ale or lager or will add additional ingredients to the boil. If a brewer is making a cherry wheat beer, for example, they will put cherries in a mesh bag and add those. If the brewer is somewhat less demanding of the beer's final flavor, a liquid flavor extract will be added. The brewers with the highest standards generally shun extracts because they often have a phony taste and emit a whiff of laziness. Russell Springsteen, owner of Right Brain Brewery in Traverse City says it most succinctly: "Extracts are for sissies."

It's time to move the wort from the boil kettle to the fermentation vessel. At this point, brewers want to bring the temperature of the wort down rapidly to prevent the production of additional dimethyl sulfide, which is also known as DMS. Dimethyl sulfide is a natural byproduct of the brewing process; it is produced in mashing and fermentation, and there's no way brewers can prevent it. A small amount of DMS in beer—particularly lagers—is desirable, but too much can make beer smell and taste like creamed corn. Running the wort through a heat exchanger to cool it rapidly stops the production of DMS. (The best example of a beer containing high levels of DMS is Rolling Rock.)

Now a brewer will measure their beer's gravity. You've probably heard people refer to "high-gravity beers" and may not have understood what the term means. Even though a "high-gravity beer" sounds cool, it's more important to the brewer than it is to you as a drinker. A beer's gravity merely refers to the weight of the wort compared to the weight of water. In other words, it's a measure of how much stuff is dissolved in the liquid. Measuring gravity throughout the brewing process is particularly important when developing a new recipe; good record keeping helps to ensure a consistent product or aids in tweaking subsequent batches.

Now that the beer has been cooled below eighty degrees Fahrenheit and the wort has been moved from the boiling kettle to the fermentation tank, it's time to "pitch" the yeast. There's a saying in beer making: brewers make wort; yeast makes beer. There's a lot of truth to that adage, but knowing which yeast to add to the wort is the brewer's next trick. Lagers are usually made with the *Saccharomyces pastorianus* yeast. Ales, on the other hand, are most often brewed with the *Saccharomyces cerevisiae* yeast. Although *S. cerevisiae* is commonly called "brewers yeast," it is also used in winemaking and baking.

Notice anything interesting about the name *Saccharomyces cerevisiae* itself? Breaking it down from the scientific name, which is Latin derived from Greek, *Saccharomyces* translates roughly to "sugar mold," while the root of *cerevisiae* comes from Latin and roughly translates to "of beer." Maybe "sugar mold of beer" doesn't exactly sound yummy, but remember that yeast *is* a fungus.

The *Saccharomyces pastorianus* lager strain works its fermentation magic best at lower temperatures, and as fermentation nears completion, the yeast tends to settle at the bottom of the fermentation vat. Ales, on the other hand, are top fermented, which means that during fermentation the yeast tends to rise to the top, producing a rich foam that needs to be vented.

S. cerevisiae is the most common type of yeast used in brewing ales, but brewers can choose from among several different strains. The choice of yeast helps to determine the beer's flavor because yeast is a living organism and each strain has its own metabolism, and part of what it does—besides converting sugar into alcohol—is create additional chemical compounds that add flavors that taste like green apple and other fruit, cloves, or rotten eggs. Most American ales tend to have their yeast flavors hidden by copious hops, but Belgian-style beers are best at letting yeast flavors through.

Yeast is the Rodney Dangerfield of brewing. When Joe Beer Drinker talks about aroma or flavor or head, he credits the malt or hops; yeast, it seems, doesn't get any respect. But brewers know that yeast is the most important ingredient in beer because it influences every aspect of the product, and it's difficult to cover up the sulfur-like smell, what brewers call an "off flavor," when yeast doesn't behave properly. And yes, *behavior* is the right word, because brewing yeasts are living single-cell creatures that perform a Jesus-like miracle of turning sugary water into beer.

"Brewers are yeast wranglers," says Andy Largent, the brewer at the Filling Station in Traverse City. If you get a craft lager straight from the tap with a sulfur-like smell to it, Largent says, it's usually because the brewer hasn't been able to get the yeast to behave properly.*

One of the best ways to get yeast to behave properly is to ferment the beer at the proper temperature. Ales are generally fermented at between sixty and seventy degrees, lagers between fifty and sixty degrees. Beers fermented at higher temperatures usually produce all kinds of nasty tastes and smells—with a notable few Belgian-style exceptions that are fermented upward of ninety degrees. The fermentation time for lagers is longer because they are fermented at lower temperatures.

Far too often, brewers fail to treat their yeast with respect, and when that happens, Emily Geiger is likely on the receiving end of an angry phone call. Geiger is the staff microbiologist at Keweenaw Brewing Company in Houghton and one of the founders of Craft Cultures, which is Michigan's only yeast provider.

When Geiger gets a call from an angry brewer who says that they just brewed a bad batch and it's the yeast's fault, she walks the brewer through a series of checks to isolate the problem. The brewer's anger quickly fades when they realize the problem is usually mechanical in nature. "It just kills me," Geiger says. "When recipes go wrong, [brewers] always blame the yeast first. That's how it goes, because it's the only thing that's dynamic in their systems."

Geiger's fledgling company is quickly growing in importance to Michigan's brewers because it provides the missing ingredient to a

Emily Geiger, founder of Craft Cultures in Houghton, prepares a solution to trap wild strains of yeast. Craft Cultures is Michigan's only yeast provider for the brewing industry.

A yeast "trap."

---

* During the writing of this book, my wife and I paid a casual visit to a (different) brewery in Traverse City. When my wife ordered the brewery's lager, she immediately noticed a distinct smell of sulfur. We called the server over and told her that the beer smelled bad and she should not serve it. The server smelled it and said, "No, this is what it's supposed to smell like." It was a disappointing example of a brewer believing that he was making a good beer—and the staff not knowing any better.

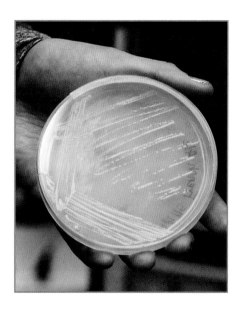

Once the yeast has been trapped, it is grown in a petri dish so Geiger can isolate and identify the strain.

one hundred percent Michigan-produced beer. The idea of "Michigan yeast" might be a little overstated because yeast is universal. The air you breathe contains tiny amounts of yeast, and many of the strains sold by a Michigan supplier are going to be the exact same strains that brewers have used around the world for centuries. But Geiger offers Michigan brewers something other brewers have never had before: new strains of yeast—UP Lager, Keweenaw Ale, and Eagle River Ale—trapped in Michigan by Geiger herself.

Trapping yeast?

Now, before you imagine Geiger putting on her Stormy Kromer and red-and-black plaid wool jacket, grabbing her shotgun, and heading out into the northern Michigan woods to stalk wild yeast, you should know it doesn't work quite that way. She's a microbiologist, after all, and her big game is very small and the process is pretty passive. To trap yeast, Geiger prepares a jar in the lab before she heads out. She half fills the jar with wort and then covers the open end of the jar with a couple layers of cheesecloth. The cheesecloth will prevent large debris from falling into the jar but will allow microscopic organisms to enter. Then she puts the jar out in a remote location—on a riverbank or lakeshore—and lets the wind blow yeast into the jar. Five days later, she collects the sample and brings it back to her lab.

Using basic lab techniques she learned as a student at Michigan Tech, Geiger separates the yeast from the bacteria and other stuff and then begins to look for yeasts that are suitable for brewing. Lager yeasts are particularly easy to find because they contain a quickly identifiable enzyme—β galactosidase—that is not found in yeast strains used to brew ales.

Once Geiger identifies a yeast strain that looks like it could be used for brewing, the next question becomes, "How does it *taste*?" The only way to tell if a strain is good for brewing is to make beer with it. Taking a chance with her first batch of trapped yeast, Geiger asked a home-brewing friend to make a one-gallon batch of beer. "We were all amazed," Geiger says. "It was so palatable, so unique."

That experience gave Geiger courage to trap more yeast and, more important, show brewers what these new strains of yeast can do. A few months later, she took three batches of beer, all brewed from the same recipe but with different strains of trapped yeast, to a meeting of the Michigan Brewers Guild for a side-by-side taste test. One strain made the beer taste light and crisp like a lager. Another made the beer taste like a saison—a style of beer known for its somewhat fruity or flowery taste and smell. The last strain imparted a clove flavor to the beer. The brewers were impressed and the orders started flowing in.

As far as Geiger knows, she is the only yeast distributor in the world who is providing new strains. And after collecting three strains from near Lake Superior, she began to collect yeast strains from other parts of the state so that she could offer a complete Great Lakes series.

⇒≫≫≫⇒

Now that the yeast is doing its thing and the wort is fermenting into beer, there's another chance to enhance the liquid by "dry hopping." This is a technique the brewers at Stroh's never dreamed of. Even though it might sound like it's something a brewer does while jumping on one leg, it's simply the name for the process of adding hops during fermentation. The primary goal of dry hopping is to add additional aroma to a beer. But, if not done correctly, there's a risk that a brewer could ruin the batch. Hops are not sterile, so adding them after the boil increases the chance that the brewer will introduce undesirable bacteria that will induce ugly, unwanted flavors. The fear of ruining a batch forces brewers to wait until late in fermentation—when the alcohol level is high enough to kill any bad stuff—to dry hop.

A good example of a beer that has been dry hopped is Crooked Tree IPA by Dark Horse Brewing Company; one sniff is all you need to pick up on its citrus and pine-like aromas. Dry hopping enhances beer because esters, which give hops their flavors and aromas, often evaporate or chemically change in the intense heat of the boil. The best way to make sure the beer doesn't lose those hoppy esters is to add them when the liquid is at room temperature.

But something else happens during the fermentation process that's bad—really bad. While the yeast is converting the sugars to alcohol, it's also producing an undesirable chemical—$(CH_3CO)_2$, which is more commonly known as diacetyl. Diacetyl (pronounced "di-uh-seetl") gives beer a flavor that can most closely be compared to movie theater popcorn. A little bit of diacetyl is desirable in an ESB (extra special bitter), but in a lager it's deadly.

Diacetyl is the bane of brewers. Even the best brewers occasionally have a diacetyl problem because it can exist in pipes, hoses, and pumps and can contaminate several batches before it's discovered. Brewers have a choice to make if they discover diacetyl in their beer: either serve beer that tastes like popcorn or throw it out. Ironically, the best way to avoid diacetyl is to make sure fermentation is complete because even though yeast produces diacetyl, it will also absorb the chemical as fermentation winds down.

Fermentation is done, and our liquid is now essentially flat beer. So the next question is, "How do we add bubbles? The first thing we do is move it from the fermentation tank to the conditioning tank, and then pump in a gas until the liquid is saturated.

After wort has fermented into flat beer, the liquid is transferred into brite tanks for carbonation and then into kegs for sale by the glass.

The vast majority of beers are saturated with carbon dioxide, but nitrogen is growing in popularity. Adding nitrogen results in a beer with tiny bubbles that swirl around a glass until they coalesce in a rich head. Besides the entertainment value of watching this seductive show, nitrogen makes Saugatuck Brewing Company's Neapolitan Milk Stout go from really good to amazing because it gives a beer a creamier mouth feel.

The level of carbonation varies among styles. Traditional English beers have almost no carbonation, while some German *weizens* (wheat beers) are so highly carbonated that you may have to let the beer settle two or three times during a twelve-ounce pour from a bottle.

Now, many of us developed our beer knowledge back in our college days, and we probably all remember from the morning after that wild party that there are few things worse than flat beer. (Okay, maybe that pizza that was kept at room temperature for ten hours is worse, but not by much.) But maybe carbonation isn't all it's cracked up to be. Carbonation adds a sharpness to beer that robs it of some of the flavors. And forced carbonation is only a fairly recent development, widely adopted after the end of Prohibition. Before Prohibition, beer likely would have been served to you straight from the cask with the only carbonation being the byproduct of fermentation. That type of beer is making a comeback under the banner of "real ale."

Real ale is made by putting the beer in a wooden or aluminum cask and allowing it to continue its fermentation for another two or three weeks at fifty to fifty-five degrees Fahrenheit. There's no need to add more yeast, but at this point the brewer can add additional hops or some other flavor component, says Jack Archiable, the beer historian and jack-of-all-trades at Short's Brewing Company. (Brewers at Short's will usually add something like chestnuts, chocolate, or licorice to one of their IPAs to give it a twist.) The beer is then hand pumped from the cask to glass using a "beer engine," a pump invented in the late 1600s. Because the beer is so lightly carbonated, some pubs put a device on the spout called a "sparkler" that gives the beer a head of foam. Archiable says this is done more for appearance's sake than anything else. When beer is served from a beer engine without the sparkler, however, it's called "slake."

Okay, let's say you've chosen to carbonate the beer and it's now ready to be packaged. The brewer has still more decisions to make. If the product is to be packaged for distribution, the brewer faces a question of whether to put the liquid in a bottle or a can. It's a dilemma similar to the one you face at your local grocery store when the bagger asks, "Paper or plastic?"

Many consumers choose bottles over cans in the belief that metal changes the flavor of the beer and glass has more cachet since we tend to associate cans with cheap beer. Beer purists, however, say that aluminum cans are the superior choice because they do not allow light to penetrate (light spoils beer) and there's less air in a can than there is in a bottle (contact with oxygen also spoils beer). And then there are the secondary issues of breakage and weight that make cans the superior choice.

As a consumer, however, your best choice for packaging and transport might just be a reusable stainless steel growler, which holds sixty-four ounces of beer. Even though you pay upward of $25 for one up-front, it's by far the best choice for transporting your

Jack Archiable, the "brewstorian" and jack-of-all-trades at Short's Brewing Company.

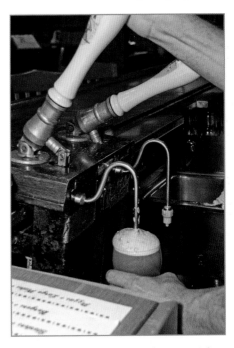

This hand pump at Grizzly Peak in Ann Arbor is used to pour "real ale," which is carbonated naturally through the fermentation process.

Because packaging equipment is expensive, many Michigan craft brewers contract for services from Michigan Mobile Canning, a company whose portable line is easily transported from brewery to brewery.

beer—and for saving the planet. Just make sure to clean and sanitize the growler thoroughly before refilling at your favorite taproom.

The final decision the brewer makes is whether to pasteurize. Stroh's was pasteurized because the heating process kills yeast and bacteria that could cause the beer to develop an unwanted flavor or smell and it gives the beer extended shelf life. But pasteurization involves heating the beer to 140 degrees after it has been bottled, artificially aging the beer and muting both malt and hop flavors.

In order for an unpasteurized beer's (like Bell's Oberon) full flavor profile to come through, however, it needs to be stored in a cold, dark place. It's easy to do that in a brewery's warehouse, but brewers cannot control the temperature of a case of beer as it goes from the brewery to the distribution center and eventually to a retail outlet. Therefore, the decision to pasteurize is a compromise that many brewers are willing to make.

A bottling line at Brew Detroit, preparing to package Atwater Brewery's Vanilla Java Porter.

All these changes in brewing have many drinkers wondering, what is *craft* beer and *microbrewed* beer anyway? Microbrewing is simply a measurement of a brewery's production. In Michigan, a microbrewery is any brewery that produces fewer than sixty thousand barrels annually. The definition of craft beer, on the other hand, is pretty murky, and the answer you get depends on whom you ask.

Stephen Roginson of Batch Brewing Company in Detroit characterizes craft beer almost poetically. "You can talk about ingredients and batch size," Roginson says. "At the end of the day, it's the love and passion that goes into the product. It's not completely driven by autopilot. It isn't run on routine. It's needs to run on soul. It's the intention behind the beer."

Dave Engbers, co-owner of Founders Brewing Company in Grand Rapids, is uneasy with the term "craft beer."

"You know, it's one of those things where people have to put labels on things," Engbers says. "To me craft beer is about the quality of the liquid. There's no question that Anheuser-Busch has the ways and means to create a great craft beer; they simply choose not to. Don't get me wrong; Anheuser-Busch, Miller, Coors—they are phenomenal brewers. Their ability to nail a recipe and the consistency across a broad spectrum of ingredients that they use is phenomenal. But to me a craft brewer is a brewer that brews beer that is full of flavor, complexity, and aromatics."

Of course, Founders, which had been considered one of the best *craft* brewers in the country, is no longer considered a craft brewer under the definition established by the Brewers Association, a not-for-profit trade organization. In December 2014, Founders announced that it was selling a 30-percent stake in the company to Mahou San Miguel of Spain. That simple investment meant that Founders no longer fit the label of "craft brewer" as defined by the Brewers Association because it was no longer less than 25 percent owned by another company.

Think that's confusing? Just wait. It gets murkier.

The Brewers Association also defines a craft beer as one "whose flavor derives from traditional or innovative brewing ingredients and their fermentation." Traditional *or* innovative? That's no help; that could mean almost anything. Is there anything more helpful, more definitive?

Well, at one time, a craft beer was defined as one that was brewed without adjuncts—wheat, oats, corn, rice, or rye. That definition was a bit of a poke at Anheuser-Busch, Miller, and Coors, which made many of their best-selling beers with corn and rice to make them lighter and crisper. The Brewers Association was forced to abandon that definition because you can't have a *wit* (Belgian wheat) beer like Bell's Oberon without a wheat adjunct. Besides, many craft brewers chafed at the definition as too limiting because it would mean there would be no Vanilla Java Porter from Atwater Brewery or double rice IPAs from Kuhnhenn Brewing Company, let alone a mind-bending Thai Peanut beer from Right Brain in Traverse City.

Some people say that the definition of a craft beer is one that is produced in small amounts. But wait! With its latest expansion complete, Bell's Brewery Incorporated is capable of producing a million barrels a year! Can brewers that make beer on that scale still be considered "craft" brewers, even if they produce innovative stouts and Two Hearted Ale, an IPA judged to be among the country's best beers? Larry Bell, the brewery's owner, believes that the definition of craft beer is slipping, and the ethos behind craft beer has as much to do with the quality of your company as a corporate citizen as it does with the quality of your beer.

Maybe the best approach to craft beer is to take an "I know it when I see it" approach. Unusual ingredients and batch sizes are indicators, but it's what's goes into the process that you can't see, smell, or taste that makes the difference. Craft beer is brewed by individuals who are motivated by a passion for excellence. It is brewed by people who refuse to be process drones. It is brewed by people who have created a culture that values quality over quantity, individuality within a community, and equal parts tradition and innovation. It is brewed by people who are constantly looking for ways to improve in the pursuit of perfection.

So here we are at a time and place in brewing like no other. Creativity and experimentation are giving us radical new flavors, but Michigan's brewers are dipping back in time and reviving some of brewing's oldest traditions. Perhaps at this point it would be helpful to ask, "How did we get here?"

AN INDUSTRY REBORN

Michigan is today the Great Beer State because of the contributions of many people, but of one man in particular.

Ben Edwards was a bit of an unusual character in that he was always looking to challenge himself to try something new and different. In 1965, the high school English teacher bought a rough-and-tumble bar at the corner of West Canfield and Second Avenue in Detroit's Cass Corridor, closed it down, remodeled it, and reopened it as the Traffic Jam and Snug.

Edwards's restaurant evolved over the next twenty years, and by the late 1980s—even though the neighborhood was slowly dying from the influence of drugs, prostitution, homelessness, and decay—the establishment was still popular with professors, politicians, urban pioneers, and a few suburbanites. The Traffic Jam was an early example of what would become today's locavore farm-to-table movement. Besides the restaurant, Edwards owned a bakery and dairy that supplied him with ice cream and unusual and delicious breads and cheeses. But Edwards longed to provide his customers with one more item that would complement the unique flavors of his breads and cheeses: fresh-brewed beer.

Only he couldn't.

Michigan law prohibited a restaurant from owning both a license to sell beer at retail and a brewing license. Every other state in the Midwest had already changed similar laws to make way for the brewpub trend. But Michigan lagged behind, and Edwards became determined to change that.

Knowing full well he was entering uncharted territory and working under the belief that it would be better to ask for forgiveness than permission, Edwards built a small brewery with a ten-barrel system in the back of his parking lot on the north side of West Canfield. Then, on September 16, 1988, Edwards asked the Michigan Liquor

IF IT WERE EASY, EVERYONE WOULD DO IT.

—BILL WAMBY, INDUSTRY CONSULTANT AND FORMER HEAD BREWER AT REDWOOD STEAKHOUSE AND BREWERY

Control Commission to grant a brewery license to his restaurant. At that time, Michigan had just four breweries: the Stroh Brewing Company, the Frankenmuth Brewery, G. Heileman Brewing Company, and Larry Bell's fledgling Kalamazoo Brewing Company.

Edwards's request to become the state's fifth brewery was denied.

That's when Thomas Burns Jr. stepped forward. Burns was a Grosse Pointe Park lawyer who would rather have been a brewer. Burns home brewed while he was an undergraduate at the University of Michigan, then became a brewer for Cartright Brewing Company in Portland, Oregon, while attending law school. After graduating and moving into private practice, Burns continued to brew for the Boulder Brewing Company in Colorado. When he was stricken with his first bout with cancer in 1984, Burns and his wife, Priscilla, returned to Michigan.

In 1989, Burns read about the Traffic Jam's attempts to get a brewing license and approached Edwards to help. Together, they sued the State of Michigan in federal court charging that Michigan's liquor law, which consisted of a three-tier system of brewers, distributors, and retailers, was unconstitutional under the Sherman Antitrust Act because it restrained trade. Burns's argument was a bit of a reach for two reasons. First, the Sherman Antitrust Act was established to *promote* trade by preventing the formation of monopolies. Second, there is a long tradition of federal courts being unwilling to intervene in what they view as state issues. Ultimately, two federal courts ruled against Edwards and Burns.

In 1992, the two took their argument to the state courts, and were greeted with sympathy—to a point. Edwards and Burns got the case as far as the Michigan Court of Appeals, but that panel concluded that any changes to the state law would be a matter for the legislature, not the courts: "It may very well be that brewpubs are desirable features on our economic and social landscapes, but this is not a question for us."[4]

The legal defeat disappointed Edwards and Burns, but they were already moving ahead with plan B: changing the law through legislation. State Representative Curtis Hertel Sr., a regular patron of the Traffic Jam, understood what Edwards and Burns were trying to accomplish and thought he could help. In 1990, Hertel introduced a bill in the Michigan House to allow a restaurant to sell beer that was made on premises. The bill, however, was opposed by the powerful Michigan Beer and Wine Wholesalers Association, and the proposal died in committee.

Even though the bill was dead, the idea was not. The following year, Hertel proposed House Bill 5407, and this time negotiations began in earnest with the wholesalers association. Hertel recalls that the wholesalers had two demands: they wanted a cap on how much beer any one brewpub could produce annually and a requirement that any brewpub that planned to distribute must do so through a distributor. In the end, the compromise allowed for an imperfect bill to pass. "It wasn't the ideal," Hertel says. "It was, however, a breakthrough, allowing the industry to begin in Michigan."

Surprisingly, Larry Bell opposed the bill because he thought it would be harmful to his established small brewery. A Kalamazoo Brewing Company spokesperson even testified before a legislative committee that the bill was unfair since it was possible for a restaurant to become a brewery, but it was not possible for a brewery to become a restaurant, and as a result his brewery would lose customers.

Nevertheless, on December 8, 1992, the state legislature passed the law—with the blessing of the Michigan Liquor Control Commission.

The law immediately changed the brewing landscape across the state. Detroit's Traffic Jam got license number one. Grand Rapids Brewing Company got license number two. In Oscoda, Dean Wiltse got license number three for his family restaurant. In Escanaba, Hereford and Hops Steakhouse and Brewpub was given license number four. In Ann Arbor, Barry Seifer made plans to open Grizzly Peak Brewing Company, and Matt and Rene Greff started to hunt for a location for Arbor Brewing Company. In Kalamazoo, Larry Bell, who already had a microbrewer's license, made plans to open a taproom.

Each of those early breweries had its struggles; in fact, Grand Rapids Brewing Company went out of business. But Michigan's beer entrepreneurs were not intimidated, and a second wave of breweries opened in the state in 1996–97. That two-year period saw Arcadia Ales open in Battle Creek, Atwater in Detroit, New Holland in Holland, Dark Horse in Marshall, Dragonmead in Warren, Mackinac Brewing Company in Traverse City, and John Pannell Brewing Company—now known as Founders—in Grand Rapids. It's also when a beer enthusiast named Rex Halfpenny established a publication—the *Michigan Beer Guide*—which has acted as the state's craft beer newspaper and bible ever since.

Ironically, Edwards didn't get a license for the brewery that he had built. The new law said that Edwards could now own a brewery and sell beer at the same location, but there was one problem: his new brewery, now called Detroit & Mackinac Brewing Company, was *across the street*; technically it was a brewery and not a brewpub, so he could not own it and have a license to sell beer at his restaurant. Edwards sold the brewery to Burns and opened his own brewery inside the Traffic Jam.

Within two years of taking over at Detroit & Mackinac, Tom Burns would die from another bout with cancer, and Burns's brewer, John Linardos, would buy Detroit & Mackinac and rename it Motor City Brewing Works.

Michigan is littered with the carcasses of breweries that started shortly after the state law was changed in 1992 and went out of business within a few years: Local Color in Novi, Big Buck in Auburn Hills, King's and Bo's in Pontiac, Copper Canyon in Southfield, Michigan Brewing Company in Webberville, Bad Frog in Rose City, Bear River Brewing in Petoskey, Fire Academy Brewery and Grill in Westland, Traverse Brewing Company in Elk Rapids, Brewbakers in Ann Arbor, the Blind Tiger in Howell, Frog Island in Ypsilanti, Duster's Microbrewery in Lawton—and the list goes on. Sadly, some of those breweries still sit empty, rotting like a discarded beer can by the side of the road.

There are lots of reasons why these breweries went belly up rather than belly to the bar. They may have tried to start out too big. Some were run by home brewers who lacked business acumen. Some had sloppy brewers who didn't understand that the failure to thoroughly clean their brewing equipment affected the taste of their beer. Some were bad restaurateurs. Some had impatient investors. Some were ahead of their time and just didn't find a market for the kinds of beers they produced.

But a handful did survive. Some because they were lucky. Or because they had a small band of loyal customers. Others because they were able to change with the times. Some owners were persistent or just plain stubborn.

Ask John Linardos about those early days at Detroit & Mackinac and you will hear stories of desperation—about how he and Tom Burns would keg beer in the morning and then drive around the city in the afternoon selling it to restaurants and party stores just to have enough money to pay the electricity bill.

Ask Larry Bell about those early days, and he'll tell you there were times when he was forced to ask his employees whether he should pay them or pay the water bill so that they could keep brewing. Steve Buszka, now the head brewer at Frankenmuth Brewery, recalls making beer for Bell in the late 1980s. He says even though things were financially bleak, there was never any question how the employees would respond when Bell approached them about the cash flow dilemma. The answer was always the same: "Pfffft! Just keep brewing!"

It took years for Ben Edwards's vision to become a reality, and it took decades for that reality to become part of Michigan's culture. Thanks to Edwards, there are now more than three hundred breweries in the state, and barley and hops have become important cash crops for Michigan's farmers, start-up businesses give beer tours in Kalamazoo, Grand Rapids, and Detroit, and there are three companies making brewing equipment in the state. "I don't think anyone had any clue what craft brewing would turn into," Bell says.

But before there was a Ben Edwards or a John Linardos or a Larry Bell, there was a brewing pioneer in Chelsea who was years ahead of his time.

The beer revolution in the United States began in 1976 when Jack McAuliffe opened what is considered the nation's first craft brewery—New Albion Brewing Company in Sonoma, California. Unhappy with American beers, McAuliffe decided to open a brewery that would duplicate the full-flavored, full-bodied ales he'd tasted while serving in Europe with the U.S. Navy. At the same time, Fritz Maytag was transforming the venerable Anchor Brewing Company in San Francisco into a brewer of ales, porters, and barley wine in what would become the first microbrewery in the United States. Soon the microbrewing trend would spread from California to Oregon and Colorado.

The Midwest got its first taste of microbrew in 1982, when the Real Ale Company opened in Chelsea. Looking back, brewer Ted Badgerow admits his baby brewery was destined to fail.

Ted Badgerow, brewer at Ypsilanti Ale House, was Michigan's first craft brewer, opening the Real Ale Company in Chelsea in 1982.

Badgerow said his brewery had no problem selling beer; he sold everything he made. It was shipped to stores all over the state, and beer lovers snapped it up; people came to Chelsea from all over the region just to have a glass and check out the operation.

But before the brewery even opened, there were warning signs. The biggest one was a form letter from the federal government after Badgerow applied for the brewery's tax license. That letter ominously said the establishment of a brewery is a considerable capital enterprise, and anyone looking to open one should have substantial resources on hand. "But we didn't take that advice," Badgerow says with a smile.

It was the summer of 1980, in the midst of a national economic downturn, and Badgerow was working on a Michigan dairy farm that was facing hard times. At that point, the economics of farming had been turned on its head: it cost more to produce a gallon of milk than farmers could sell it for. Family farms were going out of business across the Midwest, and Gordon Averill, the owner of the farm where Badgerow was working, was considering getting out, too. As Averill and Badgerow stood in front of the nearly worthless milk storage equipment, Badgerow innocently asked how much the tanks would be worth if they were filled with, say, beer.

The conversation paused as the two began to consider the issue seriously: "What would it take?" Badgerow, a home brewer for nearly ten years, had the experience. Averill could convert his worthless dairy equipment into brewing vessels. What did they have to lose?

The two were stunned by the willingness of friends and family to invest, and they quickly raised $12,000. They found space in the building at the base of Chelsea's famous clock tower and turned Averill's dairy equipment into fermentation vats. The centerpiece of this new brewing empire was a fifteen-gallon commercial soup kettle that Badgerow got from a used equipment store in Muskegon.

The Real Ale Company was the Midwest's first microbrewery and the first brewery to open in Michigan in thirty-nine years.

Word spread quickly about this new brewery in a little town just off I-94, and the crowds came. Among them was the pop duo Hall & Oates, who interrupted their Canadian tour to stop at the Real Ale Company to buy seventy cases. Badgerow and the Real Ale Company were even featured in a July 1983 story in *Time* magazine on the emerging trend of microbrewing in the United States.

Among the people attracted to this radical new operation was a young man who made the thirty-mile trip from Ann Arbor to Chelsea and back on his bicycle. His name was Larry Bell.

"He was there just once," Badgerow recalls. "I remember him coming by. At the time we had such a rush of publicity. People were coming from as far away as Virginia and the midwestern states to see what we were doing because we were the first craft brewer in the Midwest. Some were coming for the beer, while others were home brewers who were thinking about scaling up. Some of the people who came to visit looked like they were ready to go into business right away. Larry looked like he was the least likely of those to start a business."

The Real Ale Company's success was short lived, and Badgerow admits he and Averill made two critical mistakes. First, they made unpasteurized beer that often went stale before it reached the consumer. Distributors at the time did not understand the importance of refrigeration for this unpasteurized beer. Second, it took $26 to produce a case of beer, but it was sold for only $20. "What we lacked most was any vestige of business sense," Badgerow says.

Poke Badgerow today about his experiences with the Real Ale Company and he will not snarl with anger or whine with regret.

Nor is he jealous of those who have found success and fame in the industry he pioneered. He has had a rich life since. He went on to a profitable career doing construction and laying tiles. He's also a classical guitarist and the lead vocalist for an Ann Arbor–based brass band that performs nineteenth-century music.

But now, more than thirty years after The Real Ale Company closed, Badgerow is back in the brewing business. He is a partner in Mishigama Brewing Company, which opened in December 2015 as the Ypsilanti Ale House. He's made some changes since his first approach. This time he's well capitalized, uses modern brewing equipment, and has an experienced business guy—David Roberts, a former General Motors executive—looking over his shoulder.

Of course, Badgerow had to start over with new equipment as the original equipment at Real Ale Company was liquidated when the brewery closed. Badgerow has no idea what happened to most of his old stuff, but he knows who got the fifteen-gallon soup pot. It was bought by the young man who rode his bike from Ann Arbor.

BELL'S BREWERY

Eccentric Café
355 East Kalamazoo Avenue
Kalamazoo
269-382-2332
Bellsbeer.com

OWNER: Larry Bell
FLAGSHIP BEERS: Two Hearted Ale, an IPA; and Oberon, a summer seasonal wheat

Larry Bell recalls that he started the Kalamazoo Brewing Company in 1985 with just two things: a fifteen-gallon soup pot and a modest vision. "My goal was to get to thirty thousand barrels a year, and I wanted to make $100,000 a year," Bell says. "The old-time regional brewers that I got advice from said, 'Get to that level and you will have a nice life.'"

It's safe to say that Larry Bell has exceeded that vision and has a very nice life. He owns houses in Kalamazoo and Michigan's Upper Peninsula, a condo in Chicago, and season tickets to the Chicago Cubs. Besides the production brewery in Comstock, he owns the Eccentric Café and Bell's General Store in Kalamazoo; an eighty-acre farm near Shepherd, Michigan, that grows two-row barley for the brewery; and the Upper Hand Brewery in Escanaba, which he admits is a plaything. Bell's Brewery now has an annual capacity of 1 million barrels. Only a handful of craft breweries in the country produce a million barrels or more a year.

Things are good for Larry Bell today, but it was a struggle to get here. He remembers those early days when he couldn't pay the bills and employees received IOUs instead of paychecks. There was also one six-month period when he couldn't afford to pay federal taxes on his brewery's production.

So, what saved the brewery? Bell believes that the American consumer grew up just in time. He equates the American palate to that of a person who has just turned twenty-one whose taste buds are starting to mature. The craft beer movement was part of a bigger movement of people starting to appreciate fresh, locally grown foods and demand more flavors and new experiences.

Bell became interested in beer and wine partially because his father made homemade wine. He recalls that when he was seventeen and his parents had gone out, he and a couple of buddies would drink one or two of his dad's three-hundred-bottle stock of wine—and then blame it on his older brother. On a later trip to Washington, DC, to visit that same brother, he remembers being introduced to European beers at the famous Brickskeller Dining House and Down Home Saloon.

Bell took a job at small European-style bakery in Kalamazoo, where he began working with yeast and grains. One day after work, Bell recalls, a co-worker who was a home brewer asked him if he wanted to try some of his product. Curious, Bell did, and concluded that it wasn't very good, but it was enough to entice him to try his own experiments. He bought a home brewing kit and a recipe book and started making his own.

The result? Bell opened a home brew supply store in Kalamazoo in 1983 and immediately started making plans for a brewery, which opened in 1985.

How would Bell describe the quality of that first pale ale made in his new brewery? "Crap. It was fermented in plastic garbage pails with not the cleanest yeast.* The first ten batches kissed the sewer."

Looking back, Bell now realizes that the success of the brewery was a roll of the dice. "You strap yourself into the roller coaster. There's no way to get off. You just have to keep going. You take an investor's money and you owe it to them to give it your all."

---

* "Clean" yeast means the yeast has been properly separated from the trub, which is the sediment that forms at the bottom of a fermentation tank. Brewers regularly harvest and reuse yeast from batch to batch because the yeast are constantly propagating—even in the fermentation tank. Brewers yeast can reproduce both asexually and sexually, so they may have had sex in your beer. Sorry to freak you out.

Bell has been in the business for more than thirty years. He holds the honor of owning the oldest brewery between Colorado and the East Coast. But recently he's been troubled by two shifts he's seeing in the brewing landscape. First, entrepreneurs are coming into the craft brewing industry because the segment is hot and they think they can make a quick buck. "When you start seeing urologists and lawyers jumping in because there's money in it, that's a warning sign," Bell says.

The other trend that bothers Bell is that many of the longtime brewers in his generation are now literally selling out their businesses. Recently, California-based Firestone-Walker merged with Belgium-based brewery Duvel Moortgat; another California-based brewery, Lagunitas Brewing Company, sold half to Heineken NV; Seattle-based Elysian Brewing Company was bought out by AB InBev; and Salt Lake City–based Unita Brewing Company took a large investment from a private equity firm.

Bell calls the trend "the middle of the end of the beginnings of craft beer." He continues, "I give it about two years to the end of the end of the beginnings. Folks of my generation are selling out or moving on, and all those beginning entrepreneurs are going to be gone. We have entered Craft Beer 2.0, really."

Even though Bell plans to keep the brewery in the family, he did, in 2012, use the possibility of selling out as a tactic to wrest total control of the company from minority investors. Once Bell gained full ownership, he had the documents drawn up to make sure his daughter, Laura, and son, David, would take ownership in the future.

He may be looking at the endgame, but in the meantime Bell wants to make sure that everybody knows who's in charge. "As long as I'm around, I'll be dictator for life."

MOTOR CITY BREWING WORKS

470 West Canfield Street
Detroit
313-832-2700
Motorcitybeer.com

OWNERS: John Linardos and Daniel Scarsella
BREWER: Daniel Scarsella
FLAGSHIP BEERS: Ghettoblaster, an English-style mild ale; Nut Brown Ale; Motown Bohemian Lager, brewed with four classic European hop varieties; IPA; Motor City Hard Cider

It's a summer morning, a Friday, in Detroit's Cass Corridor. The doors have been open at Motor City Brewing Works for only a few minutes, but already the place is starting to fill with customers.

There's a buzz in the air at the brewery, and the entire neighborhood is humming with activity. Down the street, people are playing with their pets at the neighborhood dog park. Across the street at the Shinola store, people are lined up on the sidewalk waiting to take a ride around the neighborhood in a two-seat Indy-style racecar. Music flows out of a window of a nearby apartment in what used to be an empty building. After years of decline, Detroit is undergoing rejuvenation, and the Cass Corridor is now one of the coolest, most vibrant places to be in the state.

Motor City Brewing Works owners John Linardos and Dan Scarsella scramble to get set up for what they anticipate will be a busy night, with lots of visitors to this tiny brewery. It's going to be a beautiful early summer evening, and the taproom and deck will soon be packed.

Many people give Larry Bell credit for starting the craft beer movement in Michigan, and much of it is deserved. But craft brewing

DAN SCARSELLA AND JOHN LINARDOS, CO-OWNERS OF MOTOR CITY BREWING WORKS. LINARDOS WAS ONE OF THE PIONEERS OF THE MICHIGAN CRAFT BREWING MOVEMENT, SURVIVING LEAN YEARS WHEN HE DROVE AROUND DETROIT SELLING BEER TO PAY THE BREWERY'S ELECTRICAL BILL.

in Michigan started as a pull-yourself-up-by-your-bootstraps industry, and this little brewery is its spiritual home. Motor City Brewing Works is the second-oldest brewery in Michigan. In 1995, John Linardos picked up the pieces of the Detroit & Mackinac Brewing Company after the death of its owner, Tom Burns, and renamed it Motor City Brewing Works.

When Linardos opened the taproom in 2001, he envisioned it as a neighborhood joint, a place that people could walk and cycle to. But the neighborhood was crumbling around him, and he struggled to pay the bills since distribution for his bottled beers was limited to just a few miles from his location.

By 2006, Linardos was tired of the struggle and decided to get out. His plan was to sell the property but hold onto the beer brands and maybe reopen in a new location. There just wasn't enough business at the taproom, and there were days, Sundays in particular, when the place was empty.

Linardos put the property up for sale but instead of selling, he ended up taking on a co-owner. Dan Scarsella was a brewer at CJ's Brewing Company in Walled Lake when he heard that MCBW was on the market and called Linardos to inquire. Scarsella didn't have the money to buy the brewery but proposed an alternative: he would come in as a partner and take over the brewing, then help build a kitchen and run that, too. His help would allow Linardos to focus on marketing the Motor City Brewing Works and create a new long-term vision.

With the introduction of food, business improved immediately. People began to come in for lunch or dinner and a beer on their way to a sporting event, even on Sundays.

Then, in late 2007, the Great Recession took hold of the American economy. By the end of 2008, the state's unemployment rate had jumped to 10 percent. But something surprising happened: even though Detroiters were feeling the pain in their pockets, business at Motor City Brewing Works continued to grow. Young professionals began to resettle the core of a city that had been abandoned by their baby boomer grandparents. They also began to demand "authenticity" in their lives; they didn't want to buy a beer based on its advertising, they wanted a personal connection to the person who made the beer.

"Authenticity" is what sets Motor City Brewing Works apart from every other brewery in the state. New breweries today are generally well financed, and many of their taprooms are cookie-cutter in design. But MCBW is a genuine we-built-it-ourselves Detroit experience. It's small and difficult to find even though it's on the same block as Jolly Pumpkin's new taproom, a Shinola store, and Jack White's Third Man Records store. It's the kind of place you like because it's small, it's cool, and customers feel like they *discovered* it and want to share with their friends. Today, the tiny taproom—with a capacity of fewer than a hundred people—is usually crammed, and it takes an effort just to get to the bathroom or the bar. Nevertheless, MCBW is an enjoyable place to have a beer because of the energy in the room—and the surrounding city. The success of the taproom and the brewery itself parallels that of the neighborhood.

"This is a genuine Detroit experience," Linardos says with obvious pride. "We built it ourselves."

ARBOR BREWING COMPANY

ABC Brew Pub
114 East Washington Street
Ann Arbor
734-213-1393

ABC Microbrewery
720 Norris Street
Ypsilanti
734-480-2739

Arborbrewing.com

ABC India
#8 Magrath Road, Allied Grande Plaza
Ashok Nagar Bengaluru
Karnataka, India
+91 80501 44477
Arborbrewing.in

OWNERS: Matt and Rene Greff
BREWER: Chris Davies
FLAGSHIP BEERS: Sacred Cow IPA; Bollywood Blonde, a blonde ale; Buzzsaw American IPA, a hop-forward, West Coast–style IPA; Ypsi Gypsi, a session pale ale

It's an understatement to say that brewing in Michigan has come a long way since 1992. Michigan beers are in demand not only throughout the state and country but now around the world. Founders, already distributing beer in Europe, is now brewing in Spain through a partnership with Mahou San Miguel. Danish distributor Drikkeriget imports several brands from Michigan, including Jolly Pumpkin, Dark Horse, Kuhnhenn, Short's, and B. Nektar.

But no one is more intimately involved in the expansion of Michigan craft beer around the world than Matt and Rene Greff, owners of Arbor Brewing Company in Ann Arbor and Ypsilanti. One February day in 2012, they found themselves sitting on the patio of their newest brewpub—in Bengaluru, India—asking themselves, "How did we get here?"

⇒⤑⤑⤑⤑

The Greffs' journey to India started when Matt and Rene were just a couple of college kids in the late 1980s. Even though the two knew each other while they were students at Kalamazoo College, they were not a couple when they traveled to Europe—Matt to Germany to study political science and Rene to eastern France to study philosophy. Separately they saw and appreciated the communities and rituals that surround beer in an older culture. Matt remembers being fascinated by the flavors and presentation of beer and being blown away when he realized that a person can't have that precious first sip without first saying, "Prost!"

Those rituals are still strong with them today. "If I have a beer without saying 'Prost!' Matt will literally go, 'Hey!'" Rene says.

The two returned from their foreign studies long before the American beer renaissance, so their search for the German beers they had fallen in love with ended in disappointment. They were able to find German beers in a handful of southeastern Michigan stores, but they didn't taste as good as they remembered; far too often they were stale by the time they hit retail shelves. Matt quickly concluded that the only way they would be able to drink the kind of beer they both wanted was if he made it himself.

In 1992, Matt found a home brewing kit at a store in Ann Arbor, started making his own, and quickly concluded that brewing was a whole lot more fun than his 9-to-5 job as a database analyst. With the change in the law that allowed for brewpubs, the Greffs began to ask, "What if?"

The couple, now both in their late twenties, started looking for a location, and when a restaurant on East Washington Street closed, they pounced on it. On July 12, 1995, Arbor Brewing Company became Michigan's fifth brewpub, opening in a one-hundred-year-old brick Victorian building just east of Main Street.

Ann Arbor buzzed with anticipation waiting for the opening of Arbor Brewing. The Greffs were in keen competition with another brewpub, Grizzly Peak, to see which would open first, and the city's beer lovers were primed.

A line of people stretched down Washington Avenue the day Arbor Brewing Company opened, but from the minute the doors were unlocked it was a disaster. The Greffs knew how to make good beer, but they knew nothing about how to run a restaurant. According to David Bardallis's book *Ann Arbor Beer: A Hoppy History of Tree Town Brewing*, the opening went so horribly that "they closed for a week to regroup before opening again—during the week of the Ann Arbor Art Fairs, the busiest time of the year: 'It was a week of the exact same nightmare,' said Matt. 'Only worse,' Rene said."[5]

Rene and Matt realized they needed to take a more hands-on approach. Matt took over the kitchen, and Rene ran the front of the house from open to close seven days a week for two straight years. They saw progress immediately, but it still took time to dig out of debt and rebuild their relationship with their patrons.

By 1998, things had improved at the Ann Arbor brewpub. Not only had the Greffs gotten their finances under control, they had a happy problem—they couldn't make beer fast enough to meet the demand. In 2002, when a delicatessen in an adjoining storefront went out of business, they added space for brewing and a banquet area.

By 2004, the Greffs began to suffer the curse of the successful entrepreneur—too much free time. They had trained a great staff and could have just sat back and enjoyed life. But they needed a new challenge. During a conversation about their favorite beer gardens in Munich, Matt suggested that they should try to bring that kind of experience to the area. Obviously they couldn't put a beer garden in their downtown location, so Rene suggested that if they wanted to create one, they might as well find a location with enough space to also build a production brewery so they could start distributing.

The Greffs made a list of all the things they wanted in a new location. It took two years to find what they wanted: an old industrial space in Ypsilanti that is slightly north of the Depot Town entertainment district, not far from Eastern Michigan University, and on the edge of a historic but up-and-coming neighborhood. It was perfect.

They built a geothermally cooled beer storage area and installed solar panels on the roof to produce the majority of the hot water used by the brewery and restaurant. It's believed to be the largest solar installation at any brewery east of Colorado.

Now, Rene looks back and realizes they're no longer kids. "There was a group of us who started in the mid-'90s," Rene says. "Today we get together and laugh and think, 'How did we all make it?'"

They may not be kids, but they seem to be just as adventurous. In 2009, they were approached by Gaurav Sikka, a University of Michigan student who was nearing graduation and preparing to head home to Bengaluru. Sikka, who had frequented the Ann Arbor brewpub during his time as a student, suggested that the Greffs should open a branch in his hometown. It would be a joint venture; Sikka would be the owner and the Greffs would be conceptual partners to help him succeed. Sikka believed that although there was nothing like an American-style brewpub in the country, there was definitely a market for one.

What was the Greffs initial reaction to Sikka's proposal? "Hell, no," says Matt. They had just opened the Ypsilanti pub and production brewery and dug their way out of debt. A new venture in India was something they just didn't need. Matt says that Rene still has stored on her computer the email she sent to Sikka, which said essentially, "Good luck, but we don't have time or the money right now."

But Sikka did not take no for an answer. He wrote back that he was willing to structure a deal any way they wanted to make it worth their while. He asked them to come to India, meet his family, and check out the market.

The next thing they knew, the Greffs were on a plane.

In India, the Greffs began a great relationship with Sikka and his family and realized that his vision for an American-style brewpub was spot-on; the tastes of a growing middle class were changing, and people were demanding better-quality foods and experiences. The Greffs worked with Sikka to determine a site, create an American-inspired menu, construct the brewery, design the decor, and train the staff. If the Arbor Brewing Company name was going to be on the door, the Greffs wanted to certain that their location on the other side of the world met the same standards for quality, sustainability, workplace environment, and local involvement as the sites in Michigan.

And when the doors opened at ABC in Bengaluru, it was a replay of that morning in Ann Arbor in July 1995—only this time they were ready. "The response to our brewpub opening over there completely floored us and our partner right out of the gate," says Rene. "You can buy a Kingfisher [beer] for $1. People are paying $5 for our beers and are clamoring for more."

The Bengaluru brewpub has a beer hall feel, with long tables that are designed for communal seating and conversation—a concept that is very unusual for India. There are no television sets at the bar, which Rene says is unheard of in India. The Greffs are not dumb, however, and they understand what's their customers want—they installed a couple of large, drop-down screens to use when important cricket matches are televised.

ABC India was so immediately successful that it took Sikka just a couple of months to decide that he also would open a production brewery.

The world has changed since the Greffs discovered beer. Back in the 1980s, the family Matt stayed with in Germany teased him about how bad American beer was. Now German brewers are sending people to the United States to learn about American craft brewing. Hops farmers in Belgium are pulling out traditional European varieties and replacing them with Centennial, Cascade, and other varieties from North America. The European Union has overturned the German beer purity laws as protectionist; now all kinds of beer—including American craft beers—are welcome there.

And a couple of kids from Michigan have a brewery in India.

ONE MORE THING: Both Matt and Rene have tattoos of the cow shown on the label of Sacred Cow IPA—Matt's on his shoulder, Rene's on her neck.

In an amazing bit of foreshadowing, in 1995, long before the couple had ever considered expanding to India, Matt gave his first IPA a prescient name: Sacred Cow. The name grew out of a *discussion* between Matt and his bar manager at the time. Matt decided he was going to brew this high-alcohol, somewhat bitter beer for himself, and didn't care if the customers drank it. The idea was greeted with considerable skepticism by his bar manager, who suggested the recipe be changed to make the beer more palatable to the public.

Matt recalls being unmoved by the appeal. "I don't care. I'm not going to change the recipe," he remembers telling the bar manager.

"So it's your sacred cow," the manager responded.

And a name was—*ahem!*—calved.

A LIQUID CANVAS

How to make a beer at the Right Brain Brewery in Traverse City: make wort by adding base malt and a bit of roasted malt to hot water. Separate the malt and the wort, bring the wort to a boil, and add some hops, sixty pounds of smoky pig bones, and a pig's head. After the boil, move the wort to the fermentation tank. Add yeast—

Wait . . .

A pig's head?

Are these guys high?

No, they're really quite sober. And Right Brain's Mangalista Pig Porter is more than a gimmick. It's a really good beer. In fact, it won the gold medal for Best Experimental Beer at the 2011 Great American Beer Festival.

Mangalista Pig Porter is indeed unusual, but not all that atypical. When it comes to beer, a handful of brewers around Michigan take a "We're going to brew it because we can" approach. While some brewers look at the four raw ingredients of beer and see a finished product that doesn't need to be adorned, others look at beer the same way an artist might look at a blank canvas and decide that painting a landscape just isn't enough. They want to do more. They want to *express themselves*, and they'll be damned if they're going to be limited to paint.

Most breweries in Michigan change their brewing schedules to feature seasonal beers or introduce new beers as a way of keeping things fresh. But for Michigan's most creative brewers, brewing schedules change because creativity is at the very heart of what they do. Sometimes they want to pair beer with food. Sometimes they're driven by curiosity and want to see what would happen if they cross a beer with their favorite cocktail or dessert. Or sometimes they just get an idea.

Michigan's brewers are national leaders in brewing innovation and creativity. Partially that's because Michiganders are hardworking,

YOU HAVE TO UNDERSTAND THE SCIENCE BEHIND MAKING GREAT BEER BUT LOOK PAST THAT SCIENCE. IF YOU ARE GOING TO TAKE SOMETHING LIKE BEER AND ELEVATE IT TO A WORK OF ART THAT EVERYONE CAN ENJOY, YOU CAN'T BE BOUND BY THE SCIENCE. YOU HAVE TO LOOK PAST SCIENCE TO THE ART. YOU HAVE TO UNDERSTAND THAT IF YOU ARE GOING TO MAKE GOOD CONSISTENT BEER.

—RON JEFFRIES, BREWER, JOLLY PUMPKIN

do-it-yourself people, and partially it's because they are surrounded by all kinds of opportunities to explore. Michigan produces more than two hundred agricultural products, which is far more than our brethren midwestern states. Unlike Ohio, Indiana, and Illinois, where agriculture is a succession of fields growing corn, wheat, and soybeans; corn, wheat, and soybeans; corn, wheat, and soybeans, Michigan produces corn, wheat, and soybeans—and apples, cherries, and peaches; blueberries, strawberries, and raspberries; tomatoes, asparagus, melons, and beets. All of those Michigan agricultural products are fodder for the imaginations of Michigan's brewers—along with maple syrup, the fruit of the paw paw tree, and the new-growth tips of spruce trees.

Of course, Michigan's brewers use lots of ingredients that aren't produced in Michigan: coffee from around the world; cinnamon and other spices from Asia; vanilla beans from Madagascar; mangos from India; and pistachios from a strange and exotic place called California.

It may not sound like it, but Michigan's brewers do have limits to what they will put in their beer. Vegetarians can relax because there's not actually a rodent in Right Brain's Flying Squirrel Brown Ale, and when the owner of Short's Brewing Company says, "We're not afraid to do crazy shit," be assured that he doesn't brew beer with excrement.

But the limits can stretch pretty far. Perrin Brewing Company in Comstock Park doesn't brew with excrement exactly, but its Blazin' Hotbox, a seasonal brown ale, comes close. It's made with South American chocolate and Kopi Luwak, which is a type of coffee made with beans harvested after they have traveled through the intestinal tract of a civet. That's right, coffee beans that have been partially fermented in the intestines of a civet, a weasel-like cat that lives in Indonesia.

Now, it may sound strange that Perrin makes a beer with civet poop, er, coffee, but people who drink civet coffee say its acidic flavor makes it the best coffee in the world. Although at between $100 and $600 a pound for civet coffee, that had better be one *damn* good cup of coffee. And for $100, you could probably get, like, three venti lattes at Starbucks.

Blazin' Hotbox evolved out of a discussion between Perrin brewer John Stewart and logistics manager Adam LeClaire. The simple question they asked themselves was, how could they take their Hotbox Ale to the next level and make it really stand out? They concluded they needed to brew it with the finest coffee and chocolate they could afford. "There's a common thread to beer inspiration," LeClaire says. "Typically it starts in a conversation where we ask, 'Can we really do that?'"

It seems that all across Michigan, that question is asked time and again, and the answer is usually the same: "Why not?"

SHORT'S BREWING COMPANY

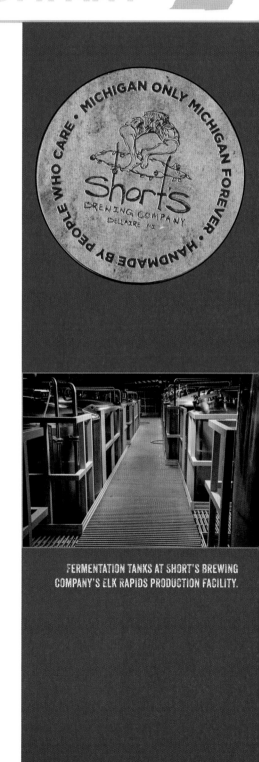

121 North Bridge Street
Bellaire
231-498-2300
Shortsbrewing.com

OWNERS: Joe Short and Leah Short
FLAGSHIP BEERS: Local's Lager; Space Rock, a pale ale; Soft Parade, a golden beer made to appeal to wine drinkers containing toasted rye flakes and pureed strawberries, blueberries, raspberries, and blackberries; Bellaire Brown; and Huma Lupa Licious, an American IPA

Joe Short's first brewhouse is in the basement of the Short's Brewing Company's pub in downtown Bellaire. Leave the noisy conversations and the clanking of glasses, plates, and silverware on the first floor and cautiously follow Short down the stairs of this one-hundred-year-old building. The rickety stairs creak under the weight of two adult men. With the first two steps it feels more like you're entering the set of a horror movie than a place that's hallowed among Michigan beer lovers.

But at the bottom of the stairs you can tell by the look on Short's face that this basement brewery is a place he dearly loves. Here in this basement, between the stone walls and under the low, wooden-beamed ceiling, is where he and his brewers imagined some of the most unusual and honored beers ever made in Michigan.

There's Bloody Beer, a light-bodied beer that glows red because it has been fermented with Roma tomatoes and spiced with dill, horseradish, peppercorns, and celery seed; it won a silver medal at the Great American Beer Festival (GABF) in 2009. There's Key Lime Pie, a beer made with limes, milk, sugar, graham crackers, and marshmallow fluff; it took gold at the GABF in 2010 and 2014. Then

FERMENTATION TANKS AT SHORT'S BREWING COMPANY'S ELK RAPIDS PRODUCTION FACILITY.

there's Melt My Brain, a golden ale that tastes like a gin and tonic cocktail. Melt My Brain is brewed with coriander, juniper berries, and limes that are blended with tonic water. It took a silver medal at the 2015 GABF.

Short leads a quick tour of the brewhouse. Wooden walls separate the brew kettles from the fermentation vats and a refrigeration unit that keeps the beer cold for the pub upstairs. Short knows every square inch of this cramped space: he designed it, helped build it, and has brewed hundreds of batches of beer here.

On one side of one of those wooden walls, a Peter Griffin doll—a character on the animated TV show *Family Guy*—hangs from the ceiling, overseeing the operations and providing spiritual guidance for the brewers. On the opposite side of the wall hang multiple medals Short's Brewing Company has won over the years at brewing festivals and competitions. The medals are obscured by hoses, a tank of oxygen, and cleaning equipment.

Nothing better describes Short's Brewing Company than the juxtaposition of the Peter Griffin doll lording it over the brew kettles while the awards hang forlornly to the side, seemingly forgotten. Griffin's character is really nothing more than an overgrown child, and in many ways the brewers at Short's are the same. The brewing equipment is their toy. Who cares about accolades when you're having so much fun?

When a visitor points out the forgotten medals, Short shrugs. "That's how we roll. We measure the success of our brewery by [the] size of our lines at beer festivals and not by how much bling we have on the wall."

Even though Short's Brewing is clearly a success, Short will tell you that he didn't start his brewery to get rich; he did it because he and his employees love making beer. That attitude is the secret behind the success of Short's Brewing Company. Short's is the fourth-largest brewer in Michigan even though it did not distribute outside the state before 2016 as the other four in the top five did.

Besides distribution, there are two other key differences between Short's and other Michigan breweries: the crew at Short's cares what you think of their beer, but they brew more to their own personal tastes than what they think will sell, and they look at the Brewers

Association style guidelines as rules for the other guys to follow.

Innovation isn't at the heart of Short's Brewing Company—quality beer is. But innovation is what Short's is known for, and the best way to understand the ideas and philosophies behind Short's beer is to hear his own words.

What's the love affair with beer?

JS: Oh, man. It's delicious. The brewing part is fascinating to me because it's infinite.

What's behind the explosion of interest in craft beer?

JS: I think it just comes down to excitement of so many different beers you can try and also to make. If you are a beer person, and a lot of us are, mostly just the excitement and rebirth—the renaissance of the handmade approach.

What is it that you do that makes you different from everybody else?

JS: We cover all the bases, so if you are looking for something more traditional or normal, we have it. If you are looking for something that's going to blow your mind, we have it. I think that what makes us Short's is we have a lot of spirit and energy behind what we do. We're a really passionate group of people who really care about it. It's not just a business plan that produces numbers. It's something that we take more serious than anything else.

Joe Short, co-owner of Short's Brewing Company, at his pub in Bellaire.

Does the beer reflect the tiny community of Bellaire at all?

JS: Yeah. In this community twelve years ago, craft beers weren't really on the scene. So we had to make a variety to bridge the gap for people who were non–brew drinkers or people who were more traditional beer drinkers, and create a palate of stepping stones to more intense and unique and diverse craft flavors.

Why do you choose to be so different? You could be following the trend and brewing IPA like everybody else.

JS: We do brew IPAs.

Well, you get the idea . . .

JS: Yeah. I didn't start Short's to make a million dollars. I started

Short's because I love making beer. The reason why we do what we do is because we love making beer. And that's what really fuels everything else. We're getting a little more mature as a company now and have a lot of investment on the line to manage, but our heart is always behind what we are inspired to make. That's why we take the approach that we take. Because brewing IPA all day is fun, but it's not as exciting as making Key Lime Pie or making Bloody Beer—you know, where you get to use fresh herbs and spices and emulsify tomatoes or use marshmallow fluff or graham cracker. It's something to get excited about between making production beers. It's like, oh, I can't wait for this one to come out. It's going to be *gooood*.

What was the first beer you brewed as a company?

JS: I think it was Local's Light. It was least expensive to make, so if I screwed it up, it wouldn't hurt us too bad.

Where does your inspiration come from? Where do you get the idea to brew with spruce tips or pistachios?

JS: You know, different days, different times of years, different experiences. There might be an experience I have with food. Beer is really food, so . . . Lots of the beers that I design are inspired by foods. I love black licorice, so I wanted to see if I could design a beer that tastes like black licorice. I love Bloody Marys. I wanted to see if I could make a beer that tastes like a Bloody Mary. You know, pistachio and cream ale just sounds good. I think that was inspired by eating some Ben and Jerry's pistachio ice cream. Other beers are inspired by ingredients that are available to us. So, like, maple syrup, for instance. It's a local product. It's fermentable. It tastes good. What else would that go with? Let's see, pecans or walnuts.

It also comes from our staff members in a much similar capacity. Like [head brewer] Tony [Hansen] made the Cerveza de Julie, which is our version of Corona. He was down in Mexico on vacation drinking margaritas one year. Some of the beers are inspired just by other ingredients that we might have come across in beers that we decided not to make, so we end up with X amount of this product or X amount of that product—well, what can we make with that? What sounds good? It's also being resourceful, too. And trying to figure out what else can top your last best creation.

What beer are you most proud of?

JS: All the beers have their own DNA, so it's just like a parent saying, "This is my favorite child." No two children are the same. There's stuff that you love about each one because they're different. It's like Spruce Pilsner—I love it because it's a lager. I love it because it's intense.

What's the craziest thing you've ever brewed? What's the most unusual thing you've ever thrown into a boil?

JS: The most unusual thing—that still didn't work out, and I want to revisit it—is bacon. Real bacon. I know people who have used flavorings. . . . Animal fats just don't work in beer.

   I would say that one of the most successful weird beers was Key Lime Pie. That wasn't my beer; that was Tony's beer. But that beer has won multiple gold medals. Any of the imperial beers—any of our specialties are their own true works of art.

There's a good deal of chemistry going on in the pot when something is boiling. There's more going on during the fermentation process. How do you ensure that those unusual ingredients aren't giving you a product that is undesirable or dangerous?

JS: I think that's where the art form comes in. As a brewer you're kind of like a chef in a way. You have to be smart about how and what you use and when you use it. Over time, we've developed certain practices that provide sterilization, and sterilization is the big key. Some wild fermentations are encouraged with other beer styles, but for us, depending on whether it's a fermentable or something that can be dissolved in the wort, like honey or molasses, that stuff goes into the pre-fermentation side. If we're using, like, an herb or something that's more like a dry hop thing, then we do have to sterilize it because we don't know necessarily where they might have come from.

Labels that will soon go on bottles are stored on a shelf at Short's Brewing Company's Elk Rapids production facility.

But throwing in unusual ingredients like spruce tips—how much of those flavors comes through? I read about a guy in Minnesota who brewed a saison with invasive zebra mussel shells.

JS: Does anybody know what zebra mussels taste like, to start? Well, that's just a cool concept, and I think that alone is going to sell the beer, but I don't think anybody is going to drink it because they want to see what the flavor of zebra mussels taste like. I think that's more an extreme marketing thing.

So, when does some unusual ingredient become something that legitimately gives beer flavor, and when does it become just a gimmick?

JS: Yeah, I guess that's really up to the consumer. They say this is the age of variety. You can go to thousands of different breweries around the country and never have two beers that taste the same. It's pretty awesome. And to think that people would want to throw a zebra mussel in there. It might provide a little dryness or bitterness, but you would never be able to pick it out of the lineup. I think the gimmicky stuff comes in when you start adding artificial flavors and you start cheating the natural process. Instead of using real strawberries you're buying extract that tastes like Charms Lollipops instead. But I think the consumers can make that distinction.

I'm willing to bet you have a really thick notebook someplace with all the recipes you've brewed. How many recipes do you have?

JS: Yeah, [we have] almost four hundred different recipes.

What is the process of developing a new recipe? Who is involved?

JS: Mostly Tony, and there is a giant list that he will populate when people give an idea. And then we go through that list and decide what makes sense from a brewing standpoint, from a production standpoint, from a seasonal standpoint. . . . If there are certain spices we can only get certain times of year, certain fruits or vegetables we can only get certain times of year. Tony is the keeper of the schedule.

How many iterations do you have to go through to get the right flavor profile?

Brite tanks in the basement brewery at Short's Brewing Company's pub in Bellaire.

JS: We haven't had anything that requires us to do anything smaller than seven barrels. Typically it's [made on the system that's in the basement of the pub], and 99 percent of the time we're successful the first go. It may take a tweak the following year or the year after that, but for the most part it's successful.

What are you tasting for when you are looking at the flavor profile of a beer?

JS: If it's something like a specialty—for instance, Spruce Pilsner—we want the spruce to be in there. We would use the spruce like we would a hop. So, I guess it just depends on if we are tasting what we thought we expected it to be. Key Lime Pie, for instance, we don't want it to be too bitter. We want it to have a soft mouth feel. We want it to touch on that graham cracker and that lime and that meringue. But we also still want it to taste like beer. I guess that's when we know.

Strawberry Short's Cake was a very interesting and relatively simple beer to develop. It was like, choose the right malts to make a cake flavor, add enough lactose to make the body full. And the strawberries are noticeable but not overpowering and it also still tastes like beer.

What attracted you to this business? Let's face it, this is not the easiest business in the world. It's capital intensive, it's long hours . . .

JS: Well, I've never been afraid of long hours. I've always gotten a lot of satisfaction from working hard and producing something that I care about. I started in the hospitality industry at a young age; I grew up working in restaurants, so that helps supply that side of the pub. When I first started making beer, it was just such a fascinating thing for me. It was a challenge to not only brew something good, but something that was outstanding. And I loved that challenge and I loved the reward of being successful at the challenge. Just like anything else, you want to repeat that process and that feeling over and over. It's like getting a sweet golf shot; you want to keep going back and getting that one sweet hit that you got. The more that you got, the more rewarded you felt. So it's a very fulfilling career for me.

In most breweries, medals won at the Great American Beer Festival are proudly displayed in public. At Short's Brewing Company's brewpub in Bellaire, the medals hang on the wall of the basement brewhouse, as if they were no big deal.

Are there any beers that you've rejected for being too weird?

JS: Not really, but we haven't made a lot of them yet, either—there's still a lot on the list.

So you have a huge list of beers someplace that you want to brew.

JS: Yeah, I've got a home brew system at home that I haven't used yet, but I've got a few that are going to be very specific to that system before we hit the pub batch with it. I just need to find the time; that's the hottest commodity going right now.

———≫≫≫≫———

ONE MORE THING: Joe Short admits that he's never done things the easy way.

Short's Brewery now occupies six straight storefronts on a stretch of M-88 in downtown Bellaire. There's a 350-seat restaurant and a store for Short's swag. The brewery's corporate offices are across the street from the brewpub in an old bank. And there's a production facility in nearby Elk Rapids.

Looking back, Joe knows he never would have gotten this far without his wife, Leah, and he credits her with saving the business. "We were so blindly ambitious that we were dysfunctional," Short says. That was when Leah stepped in and took control of the restaurant and the checkbook. That move allowed Joe to focus on making beer, fixing things in the new brewery's old building, and expanding to the Elk Rapids facility.

And just when life seemed as difficult as it could possibly be for Joe and Leah, they made yet another decision to expand—they decided to start having children. Oh, and they did one more thing a sane person would view as just plain crazy—they bought a puppy.

RIGHT BRAIN BREWERY

225 East Sixteenth Street
Traverse City
231-944-1239

OWNER: Russell Springsteen
BREWER: Sam Sherwood
FLAGSHIP BEERS: CEO Stout, a stout brewed with coffee;
Will Power, a session pale ale; Northern Hawk Owl,
an amber ale

If the brewers at Short's Brewing Company are like children playing with toys, then Russell Springsteen and the crew at Right Brain Brewery in Traverse City are like mad alchemists.

Who else would think of making a brown ale laced with peanut butter and Thai chili peppers, a cherry beer brewed with entire cherry pies, saisons made with beets and cucumbers, or a beer that tastes like Thin Mint Girl Scout Cookies?

And then there's Right Brain's most notorious creation: Mangalista Pig Porter, a smoky beer that's brewed with a Mangalista pig's head and sixty pounds of smoked bones. It won the gold medal for best experimental beer at the 2011 Great American Beer Festival.

Three things drive the bold creativity at Right Brain. First is a healthy sense of curiosity that causes the brewers to ask, "What if we try this?" The innovation could be something as simple as making the same beer with a different type of yeast, or as dramatic as pairing unusual and contradictory flavors.

Second is a desire to match beer with food, similar to the way sommeliers match wines with different types of food. That was the inspiration for Mangalista Pig Porter. Springsteen attended Pigstock, an annual culinary festival in Traverse City that's devoted to all things pork. During the event, Springsteen asked himself what

THE PUB AT RIGHT BRAIN BREWERY REFLECTS
OWNER RUSSELL SPRINGSTEEN'S ECLECTIC AND
CREATIVE PERSONALITY.

kind of beer he could make to pair with a pork dish. Which led to a conclusion that would probably not have been obvious to most of us: why not a smoky pork-flavored beer?

To make sure that nothing would be wasted, Springsteen asked for the leftover head and bones. He researched food-safety techniques and laws, and went to work making the beer. The resulting beer turned the stomachs of some—and the heads of others.

The third reason why Right Brain wants to be creative is, well, just a desire to be different. It's not just the beer. Everything about Right Brain is different. Most breweries try to locate themselves in busy downtowns, hip neighborhoods, or old buildings with character; Right Brain occupies two-thirds of a modern, one-story cinderblock structure in a Traverse City neighborhood that seems light years away from the trendy restaurants that appeal to tourists and foodies. The Right Brain taproom is one large open space filled with an assortment of tables and clutter. The walls are decorated with the works of local artists and cartoonish sci-fi illustrations, and meaningless trophies sit on a shelf behind the bar. Since employees often bring their kids to work, on summer days it can seem that Right Brain is more of a day care center than a brewery.

What's the motivation for the desire to be different? "A lot of that stems from Russ," says former brewer Nick Panchamé. "He doesn't do things the normal way."

And that may stem from the way Springsteen views himself. The name of the brewery comes from an episode during Springsteen's senior year in high school when a teacher gave her students a test to see if they were left-brained or right-brained. (Neurologists say the right side of the brain is responsible for a person's creativity and imagination, among other functions.) Springsteen was the only person in his class to be identified as right-brained.

Springsteen has long had a love affair with beer. He started drinking it in his teen years, but he admits he didn't understand, appreciate, and respect beer until he went to Germany on a competitive wrestling exchange program. He was immediately fascinated by a culture where it was possible for him—still a teenager—to sit at a bar and be treated as an adult. His next revelation came upon his return home. "Then I came back and realized our beer tasted like wet cardboard."

Cans of Will Power, a pale ale, are ready to be filled at Right Brain Brewery in Traverse City.

That's when he decided he would try his hand at brewing his own.

Springsteen's life took a turn in 2000, when he and his wife moved to the Traverse City area. Springsteen figured he would end up with a job as a barber in his new location, but he put in an application at Jack Archiable's Traverse Brewing Company. Springsteen's timing was perfect; Archiable was looking for a new brewer because his young, hotshot brewer—Joe Short—was leaving to take a job downstate.

Springsteen soon began to develop his own business plan for a combination barbershop and brewery. His first stop for financing was the local small-business development center, which told Springsteen he had to get funding from a bank. The bank immediately rejected his idea. "They thought I was crazy," Springsteen said. So Springsteen decided he would finance himself. He went back to cutting hair to make money and started buying and renting real estate. Before long, with the help of two investors, he had enough capital to open a brewery.

Springsteen chose a run-down old building on Garland Street in Traverse City's warehouse district, just west of downtown. There was only one other business on the street and parking was a problem. Nonetheless, Right Brain caught on and soon had a devoted clientele. That's when things began to backfire: Springsteen realized he was losing customers because Right Brain was *too popular*. People were coming to the door, but they couldn't get in, and Springsteen couldn't brew fast enough to satisfy demand. The decision was made to move the brewery (and barbershop) to its current location south of downtown.

(Incidentally, Right Brain Brewery had a huge positive effect on the fortunes of the section of Traverse City in which it was originally located. The area is now home to the Workshop Brewing Company, and the warehouse district is one of the city's trendiest, up-and-coming sectors, with new art galleries and housing developments.)

With the move to the new location, Springsteen began to look at the business in a different light. Initially he set out to be a home brewer writ large—no flagship beers; he just wanted to brew what he likes. But in 2011, Springsteen hired brewer Nick Panchamé, who used his culinary training at Johnson & Wales University to introduce new flavors and techniques. After graduation, Panchamé cooked for a couple of years at St. John's University Law School, then took an unpaid internship at Cricket Hill Brewing Company in Fairfield, New Jersey. Once he had enough brewing experience, he worked as an assistant brewer at 508 Gastro Brewery in lower Manhattan. After a year brewing in New York City, Panchamé took the job at Right Brain because it appealed to his left brain—it was a place where he could apply his culinary knowledge in an logical and analytical way.

Together, Panchamé and Springsteen looked at beer from a practical standpoint—what makes sense and what flavors go well together? For Schrute Farms, a saison brewed with beets and toasted coriander, it was a matter of matching up two ingredients that Panchamé says are "polar opposite" in taste. The inspiration for Hefe Cubano came from a banana milkshake with a shot of espresso that Panchamé used to drink when he lived in Rhode Island. The memory of the unique flavor combination stuck with him. Once he got to Right Brain, he knew he was in the right place to use the naturally occurring banana-like esters in a hefeweizen (a style of wheat beer from southern Germany) to make a beer that reminded him of that special milkshake.

As crazy as Right Brain's beers sound, Springsteen and says the top priority is still on the beer. In March 2016, Springsteen hired Sam Sherwood, one of Michigan's most experienced brewers, to take over when Panchamé departed for a new brewery in Ann Arbor. Springsteen hired Sherwood to improve efficiency as the brewery continues to expand and increase distribution. The move also gives Sherwood an opportunity to make beers and experiment with recipes he couldn't make at his previous breweries. They don't promise that every beer made by Right Brain will be an award-winning beer, but they do promise everything they serve has been well thought out and well made.

Springsteen, meanwhile, says that it's best to play it safe when brewing something like an asparagus beer: "We have to drink it, so . . ."

ONE MORE THING: Right Brain has the reputation of being one of the state's best incubators for young brewers, a perception that Springsteen encourages. Former Right Brain brewers have gone on to work at Brewery Terra Firma, Rare Bird Brewpub, the Workshop Brewing Company, and Beggars Brewery, among others.

JOLLY PUMPKIN ARTISAN ALES

2319 Bishop Circle East
Dexter
734-792-9124

13512 Peninsula Drive
Traverse City
231-223-4333

311 South Main Street
Ann Arbor
734-913-2730

419 S. Main
Royal Oak

441 West Canfield
Detroit
313-262-6115

Jollypumpkin.com

OWNER: Northern United Brewing Company
PRODUCTION MANAGER AND CHIEF SQUEEGEE OFFICER: Ron Jeffries
FLAGSHIP BEERS: La Roja, an unfiltered and unpasteurized sour ale brewed in the Flanders style; Calabaza Blanca, an ale aged in oak casks and spiced with orange peel and coriander; Oro de Calabaza, a strong Franco-Belgian–style golden ale with notes of pepper and other spices

Ron Jeffries is a lot like the beers he brews for Jolly Pumpkin Artisan Ales: different.

Jeffries doesn't make the coffee-flavored porters and hop-heavy IPAs that are so ubiquitous in today's brewpubs. He brews sour beers that are complex and subtle. That's not to say that Jeffries himself is sour. But like his beers, he's complex and subtle; a soft-spoken man, charming but reserved; warm and likable but not the life of the party. He's not going to be everybody's best friend, and he's fully aware that his beers won't be embraced by everyone. Jolly Pumpkin stands out as unique even among craft brewers, who are famously doing something different.

AN EMPLOYEE AT NORTHERN UNITED BREWING COMPANY IN DEXTER CLEANS A VAT AT THE END OF A DAY'S BREWING.

A workstation in the brewhouse at Northern United Brewing Company in Dexter. The brewery makes Jolly Pumpkin, North Peak, and Grizzly Peak beers.

Jeffries and his beers come from a different place and offer a different kind of drinking experience, and it's not something that everybody *gets*. Jeffries doesn't make beer; he makes art.

Yes, that sounds pretentious, but just as Auguste Rodin saw a hunk of clay and could visualize a sculpture, Jeffries looks at his raw materials and sees what will become a work of art in a bottle. Rodin was a master of balance in form, texture, and detail in his sculptures, and Jeffries looks to infuse his beer with a balance of flavors with layers that come through as the liquid moves across your tongue. Just as you may stand before a sculpture and ponder what you see, Jeffries wants his ales to leave a drinker looking deep into an empty glass.

Jolly Pumpkin was the first brewery in the United States devoted entirely to sour beers and the first to cask age all its beers. Sour beer isn't sour like a lemon, although the beers do have a certain acidity and tartness to them. At a time when most brewers are making clean, malt-forward beers or beers that are too often smothered by hops, Jeffries is creating complex beers with flavors that would cause most brewers to wonder what they did wrong.

Brewing in the modern world is all stainless steel and vacuum-sealed bags of hops, but consider this: at one time, all beer was sour beer because it was fermented in wooden casks, and there was no way to prevent unwanted bacteria and yeasts from creeping in. Brewers had a basic knowledge of malt and hops but they knew nothing about microorganisms and how to keep them out of their beer. Today's breweries invest in both physical labor and equipment designed to keep microorganisms out.

In Jolly Pumpkin's ales, Jeffries returns brewing to a nineteenth-century Franco-Belgian farmhouse tradition. The easiest and most common way to make sour beer is to ferment wort with the *Brettanomyces* yeast strain. Jeffries doesn't pitch *Brett*; he lets that particular strain—and others—find his beer naturally.

The first round of fermentation at Jolly Pumpkin's ales is done with standard Belgian yeast in large open vats. If Jeffries were to carbonate and package at this point, he'd probably have a pretty good Belgian-style beer. But Jeffries wants more, so he transfers the beer into oak casks to age for up to a year—or longer—for a second round of fermentation.

Cask aging beer is not all that remarkable. Brewers often cask age beer because the liquid draws chemical compounds from the wood that end up influencing the taste of the beer. But most brewers use casks that are generally free of yeast and bacteria.

Jeffries doesn't just want those yeast and bacteria; he encourages them and embraces them because in the end, they will give the beer the flavor he's looking for. When a new cask comes into the brewery, he will condition the cask with wort to ensure the cask picks up the bacteria and yeast that will be necessary for the next batch.

Before bottling, Jeffries blends several different batches aged separately to achieve the flavors he's looking for. Once the beer is done Jeffries refuses to do two other things that are common brewing practices: he refuses to filter or pasteurize because both processes would change the flavor of the beer.

But that's still not good enough. Prior to bottling, Jeffries adds even more yeast to allow the beer to continue to ferment in the bottles. That last round of yeast helps the ales develop the sour notes that give Jolly Pumpkin brews their distinct flavors.

Jeffries may have been the first modern brewer in the nation to brew this way, but he admits it was just a matter of time before someone did. Twenty years ago, when craft brewers were just getting geared up, it was often a challenge to get ingredients. At that time, malt was much more widely available than hops, so craft brewers made malt-forward beers. As hop availability grew in both amount and variety, brewers started to experiment with pale ales, then ESBs, then IPAs, then various hop bombs. It was inevitable, Jeffries says, that brewers would start to experiment with yeast.

As brewers go, Jeffries took an unusual route to his occupation. He was working on a master's degree in the School of Natural Resources and Environment at the University of Michigan in the 1980s when he stumbled across an old friend who offered him some of his home brewed beer. "Something in my brain exploded or melted," Jeffries says.

"I went home and I called him up and said, 'Let's start a brewery. There are these new things, these brewpubs, these microbreweries,

Brewer Ron Jeffries ages all Jolly Pumpkin products in wooden casks.

maybe you haven't heard of them, but there are these new little breweries that are starting up all over,' and he hung up on me," Jeffries remembers. "I called him back, and I'm like, 'No, look, you worked in restaurants, I could do the brewing thing. It's science, you know; I can figure it out.' He hung up again."

But Jeffries didn't let the idea go. He started studying brewing science, even though there was no program for it at the university. He began to take classes that would one day be relevant to running a brewery. Halfway through his graduate program, Jeffries was hired at Grizzly Peak brewery in downtown Ann Arbor.

His infatuation with sour beer started in the mid-1990s, when Jeffries was still with Grizzly Peak. Joel Shelton of Shelton Brothers Importing introduced him to a new Belgian beer his company was importing called Cantillon. Jeffries was intrigued with both the beer and the brewing process and decided he wanted to learn more about how the flavors were created. That turned out to be a more difficult task than he had imagined because there wasn't a lot of literature about brewing sour beer—there was far more about keeping the bacteria out of you beer than intentionally letting it in. Nevertheless, he began experimenting with sour beers at his next brewer job at Bonfire Bistro and Brewery in Northville. Store-bought cultures wasn't giving him the complexity he found in Cantillion.

Jeffries started writing a business plan for his own brewery, one that would have a Belgian flair to it. Then, one sunny, summer afternoon Jeffries and his wife, Laurie, were sitting in their backyard drinking Belgian sour beer. Jeffries said to his wife: "This beer is so complex and wonderful and tart and refreshing. If we could just make beer like this, that would be wonderful."

That's when Laurie turned to Ron and said, "Then why don't you?"

At that moment Jeffries changed his business plan: he would now open the first keg-conditioned sour beer brewery in the United States.

At the time, Jeffries says, it seemed like a no-brainer because nobody else was doing it. Jeffries and his wife formed Jolly Pumpkin in 2003 and started construction on a Dexter brewery in 2004. Less than a year later, Jeffries's beers began to win awards, including the gold medal for French- and Belgian-style ales at the Great American Beer Festival.

Despite the recognition, Jeffries encountered two problems that nearly put him out of business. First, because the beer had to be aged for a year or more, significant expenditure was required before the brewery would see its first dollar in revenue. Second, Jeffries decided he didn't want to open a taproom because he was a brewer, not a bar owner. In retrospect, he admits that was a colossal mistake because there was no direct connection—no way to educate customers about the product—and the business didn't have a daily influx of cash from the bar.

Jeffries realized that he would be unable to sell enough of this niche product through retail in southeastern Michigan to keep the brewery alive. If he was going to make it, he had to look beyond the horizon. He started distributing in Florida and a few other places, but sales remained low.

Jeffries and Laurie decided they would enter a partnership with Ann Arbor developer Jon Carlson and others, which gave them enough money to open taprooms in Traverse City, Dexter, Ann Arbor, and eventually Detroit.

That's when Dan Shelton, brother of Joel, stepped in and offered his help. "He said, 'I get it. I think I can help,'" Jeffries recalls. Soon, with Shelton's help, Jolly Pumpkin's sour beers were being sold nationally and internationally.

Jeffries believes that without the combination of Shelton's help and the taprooms the brewery would have gone out of business or be only just scraping by.

Since winning the gold medal at the GABF, Jolly Pumpkin has been recognized with multiple awards, including three first-place medals at the 2015 Hong Kong International Beer Awards. Further, Jeffries's beers were recognized by the *New York Times* in a 2010 taste test of Belgian beers:

> Our No. 1 beer was the Oro de Calabaza from Jolly Pumpkin, which, like the Good Harbor Ale, is from Dexter, Mich., a small town near Ann Arbor. A cabal of Belgian beer lovers in Dexter?

Perhaps, but these two beers were brewed by the same man, Ron Jeffries, the founder of Jolly Pumpkin, who also finds time to do the brewing for Leelanau. Both of these beers were unfiltered, giving them a hazy appearance, and aged in barrels, but beyond that they are completely different. While the Good Harbor was funky, the Oro de Calabaza was spicy, fruity and floral, with soft carbonation and fresh, vibrant flavors. Same man, different yeasts, at the least.[6]

Sales of Jolly Pumpkin's ales have improved so dramatically from the early days that in 2015 the brewery had a good problem: everything it made was selling out, so it was forced to add capacity. "I always said we would make as much sour beer as people want to drink," Jeffries says. "Now we're having to live up to that."

Because of that expansion Jeffries has been forced to take more of a management role than he has in the past, but that doesn't mean he's giving up brewing and the search for new products. "People who are different can't help but be different," Jeffries says. "I have to be creating. I have to be creating or go I'll go crazy."

SCHRAMM'S MEAD

327 West Nine Mile Road
Ferndale
248-439-5000
Schrammsmead.com

OWNER: Ken Schramm
MAZER: Ken Schramm
FLAGSHIP MEADS: the Statement, made with Traverse City–grown balaton cherries; Heart of Darkness, made from Schraammbeek cherries from Europe, raspberries, and currants; a variety of seasonal creations

Mead.

Say the word, and visions of pillaging Vikings might pop into your head. Or maybe you associate mead with a Renaissance fair where it's sold alongside deep-fried turkey legs. But you should not let its association with ill-tempered Norsemen or jugglers in foolscaps and nylon tights influence you. Mead is the oldest fermented drink in the world, and it deserves the same respect we give craft beer because it too is an artisan beverage.

For better or worse, mead is associated with medieval times, mostly because it was then the alcoholic beverage of choice since its raw materials—water, honey, and wild yeast—were readily available in northern Europe. Some people even posit that the word *honeymoon* has its etymological roots in mead. They claim that as part of a bride's dowry, the groom was given enough mead to last through a full cycle of the moon. Sounds reasonable, but it may be the medieval version of an urban legend.

Even though you've probably heard of mead, you might not be sure what it is. When mead is fermented with fruit, it is similar to wine. When it's fermented with hops and carbonated, mead resembles beer. Unfortunately, many craft beer enthusiasts tend to stay away from mead. Maybe they look askance at it because it looks and pours like wine. Maybe they avoid it because they're afraid it'll be sweet like a dessert wine. Maybe they steer clear of it because, well, in its modern versions—particularly those made with fruit and served in elegant bottles—mead might appear to be a chick

Ken Schramm, owner of Schramm's Mead in Ferndale.

drink. Okay, mead may not seem the manliest choice when you're watching mixed martial arts with your buddies, but hey, if it was good enough for Vikings . . .

For centuries debate has raged among people with too much time on their hands: is mead beer or wine? Mead's similarities to beer are obvious: it's boiled and fermented with yeast. It can be made with adjuncts to enhance its flavor and its often carbonated. But the similarity to wine is also obvious: its taste, aroma, and mouth feel are more wine-like.

Mead, however, should not have to be categorized; it deserves to stand on its own.

Just as Michigan's brewers have rediscovered beer's artisanal roots, taking that beverage to new heights, Michigan's mazers (the term for people who make mead) are doing the same for mead.

Nonetheless, even compared to the relatively small market for craft beer, the market for mead is tiny. "We like to say that if you are a big name in the mead world, you are a big fish in a Dixie cup," says Ken Schramm, owner of Schramm's Mead in Ferndale.

Still, Michigan has three big fish in that Dixie cup. In 2014 three local producers—Kuhnhenn Brewing Company, Schramm's Mead, and B. Nektar—produced twenty-seven of the top fifty meads in the world as rated by the website Ratebeer.com.[7] All three of those producers are just north of Detroit and within a few miles of each other —as the bee flies.

Of those three, Schramm's Mead is deemed the best among mead enthusiasts because its owner, Ken Schramm, is one of the county's premiere mead makers. Schramm is author of *The Compleat*

Meadmaker (2010), considered to be the bible of the craft. In addition, Schramm teaches mead making at the University of California–Davis, and has written several articles about mead making in *Zymurgy* magazine. For his work to promote and advance mead, Schramm was given the 2014 Governing Committee Recognition Award from the American Homebrewers Association.

Schramm is widely admired because, well, he makes some pretty mean mead. Here's a taste of how his meads are rated by Ratebeer.com:

Schramm's Ginger: *99*

Schramm's The Heart of Darkness: *100*

Schramm's The Statement—Reserve: *100*

Schramm's Cranberry: *100*

Schramm's Nutmeg: *100*

Schramm's Madeline: *100*

Schramm's Raspberry: *100*

Schramm's The Statement: *100*

Schramm's Blackberry: *99*

Schramm's The Rocket: *99*

Schramm's Apple: *100*

Schramm's Black Agnes: *100*

Schramm's Erik The Red: *99*

Schramm's Plum: *96*.[8]

Yeah, that's pretty good.

Schramm says there's no secret to making good mead: use simple recipes, get really good ingredients, do your best to ensure quality every step of the way, and get out of the way.

Honey is, of course, the most critical ingredient, and Schramm works to get the best he can from beekeepers in Michigan, Florida, Washington, and Pennsylvania. The only honeys he uses from outside the country are Tasmanian leatherwood honey and Scottish heather honey. Just as different styles of malt impart different flavors to beer, different styles of honey—orange blossom, clover, alfalfa—lend special flavors and aromas to the mead.

And just as there are multiple styles of beer, there are many kinds of mead. Just as craft beer can go from the lightness of a kölsch to the chewy boldness of a bourbon-barrel aged Scotch ale or an imperial stout, mead can range from completely dry to dessert sweet and from uncarbonated to champagne-like.

Schramm prefers to make meads that are big, rich, and fruity. At St. Ambrose Meadery in Beulah, Kurt Jones is making mead with all kinds of berries. Vander Mill in Grand Rapids specializes in cyser, a mead made with apples. Arktos in Grand Rapids makes a mead with pumpkin, cinnamon, and ginger. Acoustic Draft Mead in Traverse City makes meads that are lightly carbonated and tend to be lower in alcohol content than most, making them drink more like beer.

Because not that many people make mead, the knowledge base isn't as deep and there aren't nearly as many recipes as there are for beer. Schramm says that forces the typical mead maker to do some experimentation and be more creative to extract the best flavors from fruits and spices and then establish rules for fermentation.

The best flavor combinations, Schramm believes, are ones that mingle spices or high acidity with the fruity, sweet characteristics from the honey. "We're looking for a level of delicious that will make people push back in their seat," he concludes.

⟫⟫⟫⟫

Schramm began making mead in 1988. He was (and still is) a beer lover and home brewer. He got started making mead when he read the appendix to Charlie Papazian's book *The Complete Joy of Home Brewing*. His first attempt to make mead was a raspberry barkshack ginger—straight from Papazian's book—that was made with too much corn sugar and fermented way too long. "It was horrible."

But Schramm was determined to improve. He contacted Bill Pfeiffer, a brewer and mead maker who lived in Wyandotte before his death in 2000. Pfeiffer had been named American Homebrewers

Association mead maker of the year in 1985 and was one of the first five certified mead-tasting judges in the country. Pfeiffer was glad to take on a young apprentice, and Schramm has been busy as a . . . mazer ever since.

PSYCHO BREW

300 W. Greenville West Drive
Greenville
616-204-2498
Psychobrew.com

OWNERS: Chris Breimayer and Pat Breimayer

Michigan makes beer, but Michigan also makes stuff that makes beer.

The state is home to three companies that make and install brewing equipment, GW Kent in Ypsilanti, Craftwerk Brewing Systems in Lake Orion, and Psycho Brew in Greenville.

When one of the choices has a name like Psycho Brew, you didn't really think I was going to write about GW Kent or Craftwerk, did you?

Chris Breimayer, who co-owns Psycho Brew with his brother, Pat, says the business is so named for a reason: "We have an unconventional way of doing things."

Indeed, they do. Start with their history. Chris and Pat founded Psycho Brew in 2010 after two happy accidents. In 2008, Chris designed a ten-gallon brewing system and asked Pat to build it. It was no big deal for either of them as Chris has a background in architecture and the tool and dye industry, and Pat was at that time a millwright. Impressed with their own creation, they posted a photo of their system on a home brewing forum, Probrewer.com, as a "hey-look-what-we-did" lark.

That's when the second happy accident occurred. A retired banker from Ohio saw the Breimayers' system on the website and asked the brothers to build a custom *one-barrel* system for him. And then they got another email request to build a system. And another. "It was crazy," Chris says. "We were nobody."

PSYCHO BREW CO-OWNER CHRIS BREIMAYER INSPECTS A LABEL THAT WILL GO ON A BREW KETTLE OR FERMENTATION TANK.

A Psycho Brew employee inspects a seventy-five-gallon brew kettle.

Those requests made the Breimayers realize they had an opportunity to service a niche market: no other manufacturers of brewing equipment were making anything smaller than a 3.5-barrel system. In 2010, the brothers decided it was time to go into business officially, and they founded Psycho Brew, Michigan's only manufacturer of nano-brewing equipment. Their decision to build nano-systems was a critical boost for small brewers everywhere, because at last they had affordable, space-saving alternatives.

Pat took over the fabrication side of the business, and Chris took charge of sales. For the first two years the business struggled from two problems that can kill any entrepreneur's dream—poor sales and lack of facilities. Initially the two worked out of Chris's garage in Greenville—until Chris's wife decided it was time for them to go elsewhere. They moved the welding operation to an in-law's pole barn but kept the drilling and other small work in the garage. But that meant a good deal of time was wasted running back and forth between locations.

Sales began to improve, but the brothers were still plagued with location issues: should they attempt to find more space locally, or was it time to move the operation? The decision was fairly easy. Pat and Chris gained space by farming out some of the welding operations to a nearby fabrication company and started renting space in a small industrial park just south of downtown Greenville. And instead of moving closer to Grand Rapids to take advantage of the resources of a big city, the Breimayers decided to stay in rural Greenville and conduct their business over the Internet. Unconventional, yes, but Chris says this is where they want to be.

The Breimayers aren't the only people who think their business is unconventional. Chris says the brothers hear regularly from their accountant and banker about their, um, *unusual* business model. Nevertheless, it appears to be working. Unlike other businesses that take out loans in order to get big fast, Chris and Pat used their own money to avoid going into debt. And for the first three years, every

Psycho Brew fermentation tanks ready to be shipped to customers.

dollar they made was reinvested in the business. Now Psycho Brew has nearly $3 million in sales annually.

Of course that's small potatoes compared to some of Michigan's other manufacturers of brewing equipment that supply big, well-known operations nationwide. But although Psycho Brew's résumé isn't nearly so impressive, it has supplied equipment to the Filling Station in Traverse City and Bad Brewing in Mason, among others. That's Psycho Brew's niche; the company provides brewing systems ranging from 2.5 up to 15 barrels to small brewers. Not only is the company filling a niche, it's providing products small brewers can afford. Psycho Brew's most expensive systems top out at around $22,000, while its nearest competitor's much larger systems start at $60,000.

There's one more unconventional aspect that sets Psycho Brew apart: the systems themselves. Because small brewers are often forced to do more with less, Psycho Brew's systems are set up to brew double batches. The brewer can either blend the two batches into the same fermentation vat or brew two different beers at the same time. "As far as I know, there is nothing else like that out there," says Chris.

Even though there's not a big market for small systems, Psycho Brew's reputation is growing and the brothers are selling everything as soon as they make it. Orders have come from as far away as Canada, Mexico, the Caribbean, and Europe. Chris thinks he and Pat can ride this wave for another ten years.

"Really," Chris says, "all we wanted to do was to sell enough so we had money to make beer."

3

COOL PLACES

Drive north on I-75 from southern Michigan and walk into Paddle Hard Brewing in Grayling. If you didn't know that you are in northern Michigan, you know it now.

The taproom feels like a rustic lodge on the AuSable River; the interior is made mostly from exposed brick, corrugated metal, and knotty wood combined with an unfinished ceiling. It's a pleasant respite for a weary traveler.

But there's something else about Paddle Hard—something that goes beyond its interior. There's some mystical quality at work. Even though owner Dave Vargo sells beer from other Michigan breweries along with his own, all the beer sold here seems to taste extra delicious.

Paddle Hard is an example of how the design, decor, or location of a brewpub or taproom can enhance the quality and flavor the beer it serves. It sounds absurd, but brewers universally say that perceptions have a huge impact on how a drinker tastes their beer. When we're in a special place surrounded by history, interesting architecture, or good design—or just with good friends—a beer's flavor is somehow enhanced.

Paddle Hard is one of a growing number of Michigan brewpubs and taprooms that have eschewed the generic in favor of embracing the histories and cultures of their locations. Other taprooms reflect the eclectic and unusual personalities of their owners. One is in an old church, and another one opens early for breakfast. And then there's one that has won eighteen major awards and you've likely never heard of it. They are all some of Michigan's coolest places to have a beer.

PIGEON HILL BREWING COMPANY

500 West Western Avenue, Suite 1
Muskegon
231-375-5184
Pigeonhill.com

OWNERS: Joel Kamp, Michael Brower, and Chad Doane
BREWER: Chad Doane
FLAGSHIP BEERS: Walter Blondale; Shifting Sands IPA, a medium bitter IPA with a copper-orange color; LMFAO Stout, an oatmeal stout with nitrogen; Renegade IPA

You know how there are places that you like just because you feel comfortable there? That's what Pigeon Hill is for me.

Like many breweries, Pigeon Hill has that exposed brick and industrial HVAC look. But the taproom is just one room—not too big and not too small. The bar has a rough-hewn wood façade. The tables are made from old-growth white pine, salvaged from Lake Muskegon after sitting underwater for more than a hundred years. The light fixtures were salvaged from two local factories and a bowling alley. The floors are terrazzo, reflecting the building's past as a Buick dealership.

But what makes Pigeon Hill special, so welcoming to patrons, is its nod to history and its commitment to community. The northeast wall is covered by super-enlarged black-and-white photos of downtown Muskegon in its early nineteenth-century glory, when the city was a bustling port that shipped wood and other raw materials to Chicago, Detroit, Cleveland, and Buffalo.

Even though Pigeon Hill seems like a mishmash of stuff and styles, it's more than the sum of its parts. Its space works because it is functional—it is designed as a community gathering space where customers can move tables and chairs around to meet the moment.

THE BREWHOUSE AT PIGEON HILL BREWING COMPANY IN MUSKEGON.

Taps and beer menu at Pigeon Hill.

The wood and brick tones make it a place that welcomes warm conversation over a cold beverage. Best of all, there are no TVs to distract or curtail the conversation. Co-owner Michael Brower says that the goal was to give Pigeon Hill a vintage, pre-Prohibition feel, when taprooms and bars were the equivalent of a community center or a neighborhood club.

Pigeon Hill is a result of the collaboration of its three owners, Brower, Joel Kamp, and Chad Doane. All three contributed to the interior, with Doane bringing a background in furniture design. But it was a stroke of luck that brought them the very cool tables made from two-hundred-year-old white pine. As Kamp, Brower, and Doane were designing their taproom, they got a call from a local watershed preservation and conservation group that had discovered massive amounts of virgin white pine that had been at the bottom of Lake Muskegon for one hundred years. The wood—some large logs and some rough-cut timber—had fallen off a dock and was never recovered. The members of the conversation group decided to offer some of the wood to the owners of Pigeon Hill because they had heard about the brewery's desire to design an interior that would connect patrons to the city's history.

But there was a catch: the wood was free—if the bar's owners could move it from the shore. The wood had taken on so much water after a century of submergence that it was considerably heavier than it would have been otherwise. Nevertheless, the three jumped at the opportunity because of the wood's symbolism and its excellent quality. The pressure of the water had compacted it, making it harder, and the beauty of the wood's grain just can't be found in second-growth pine.

The three rounded up as many volunteers and trucks as they could to move the wood, then Kamp used a connection with another local business to kiln dry and mill the wood into usable boards. "We spent a lot of nights drinking beer and building tables," Brower says.

Pigeon Hill's location on the south side of downtown makes it a walkable destination in summer and a comfortable gathering spot to sit and watch the snow pile up in winter. "In the winter with the doors closed, everybody huddles in for warmth, talking together," Brower says. "It has a wonderful kind of communal feel."

Brower recalls with astonishment one snowy night in 2015 when two people snowshoed to Pigeon Hill from a mile away. Everybody applauded when they came through the door, covered in snow. "It's rare that people come in here and just sit," Brower comments. "People come in and talk with one another. And that was exactly the goal. We want it to feel like home."

Besides designing a brewery that would bring people together, the three partners decided they wanted to be a catalyst to help revive a moribund city, and it seems they've had some success. In just the couple of years since the brewery opened, Brower has seen a new vitality in the area, with new families moving in and new houses being built. Brower points to a new pizza place in the same building as the brewery. There's a new hot dog place nearby, a new farmers' market downtown, and several other developments in the works. That's not to mention Pigeon Hill's own $1 million investment—a new production brewery in a shuttered bowling alley just a short walk up Western Avenue. "I know it's getting harder to buy commercial real estate. That in itself says something."

Michael Brower, one of the owners of Pigeon Hill.

BRITE EYES BREWING COMPANY

1156 South Burdick Street
Kalamazoo
269-220-5001
Briteeyesbrewingco.com

OWNERS: Shelby and Brian Pierce
BREWER: Brian Pierce
FLAGSHIP BEERS: Dagwood's Wife, a blonde ale; Fearless the Idiot, an IPA; Rooibos, an amber ale made with lemon chiffon rooibos tea

Brian and Shelby Pierce didn't start out with the idea of serving breakfast and beer. The original concept for their business was a coffee shop that serves beer and a brewery that serves coffee—and it would be open afternoons and evenings.

Brian wanted a microbrewery, but Shelby—a nondrinker—wanted to offer an artisan experience for designated drivers and nondrinkers, thus the coffee. They pictured their brewery/coffee shop as a place where people could come and have a beer with friends or a cup of coffee while reading a book or working on their computers. It would be a combination of barley and beans, malts and grounds, and the people who poured wouldn't be called baristas; they would be *beeristas*.

They found the perfect location in a former women's clothing boutique at the corner of South Burdick Street and Crosstown Parkway—an unusual and slightly funky building that screams 1950s architecture. When they looked around the area, they quickly realized that they should rethink their idea. The location was just south of downtown Kalamazoo, directly across the street from a county courthouse and the city's public safety department and down the hill from a major regional medical center. If they were

BRITE EYES BREWING COMPANY IN KALAMAZOO HAS AN UNUSUAL BUSINESS MODEL. IT'S BOTH A BREWERY AND A COFFEEHOUSE THAT'S OPEN FOR BREAKFAST.

going to be a coffeehouse, the location demanded that they should be open in the morning for people going to work.

But when they opened their doors in August 2015, they realized that many of their early-morning customers were cops and hospital workers *going home* from work, and they were looking to have both breakfast (because it's morning) and a beer (because it's the end of their work day).

And the concept of eggs and kegs was born.

Brite Eyes opens for breakfast at 8 a.m. Wednesday through Saturday, and at 10 a.m. on Sundays. After a year of opening at 7 a.m. every day of the week, Brian and Shelby were forced to make the difficult decision to cut the number of hours; the staff was just being stretched too thin and something had to give. Now the brewery is closed on Mondays and Tuesdays to give Brian time to make beer, and the evening hours have been extended a bit to give customers time to consume it.

People come in throughout the day to sit and chat. At any one time there might be tables filled with senior citizens, off-duty cops, a Bible study group from one of the nearby churches, or a book group talking about that month's read.

Brian and Shelby Pierce, owners of Brite Eyes.

They're attracted by the consumables, but they're also drawn by the feel of this hybrid business. Brite Eyes seems more like a vintage 1950s diner than anything else. Brightly colored red, yellow, orange, green, and blue gray panels on the walls above the window provide color without being imposing. There's a mishmash of taps and coffeemakers behind the bar, and the open kitchen is a mixture of brewing and cooking equipment. There's a gently curving balcony overhead that serves as Shelby's office and helps to give the space a more intimate feel. The tables are made from old butcher blocks, and the windows reach from the floor to near the ceiling, letting in light and bringing an outdoor feel indoors.

"It's a great space," Brian says. "We looked at a lot of spaces and knew this was the right place as soon as we walked in. We wanted high ceilings and lots of windows. We want it to be light and bright. We want it to be as much a brewery as it is a coffeehouse and vice versa."

Despite the happy accident that came with the location, Brian and Shelby have carefully calculated their plans for the brewery. They started small intentionally. They'd seen many area breweries start out with big grand-opening celebrations, only to quickly run out of beer, killing their business. The Pierces built their business incrementally. After opening they added a wine and mead license. Then they built a patio on the lawn facing the intersection and added dinner and children's menus. And only after that did they grow from a one-barrel to a three-barrel brewing system.

That calculating approach has extended to the brewery's hours—it closes at 11 p.m. on weeknights and at midnight on weekends. One thing Brian and Shelby knew when they decided that theirs would be a brewery that served breakfast was that they would need to get up early, ready to go to work with Brite Eyes.

TAHQUAMENON FALLS BREWERY & PUB

Tahquamenon Falls State Park
M-123
Paradise
906-492-3300
Tahquamenonfallsbrewery.com

OWNER: Lark Ludlow
BREWER: Lark Ludlow
FLAGSHIP BEERS: Black Bear Stout, a drinkable stout on the lighter side; Porcupine Pale Ale, a smooth, slightly hoppy beer; Blueberry Ale, a beer made for the annual Paradise Blueberry Festival; Falls Tannin, a red

There may be no better place to drink a beer in our great state than outside on the deck at Tahquamenon Falls Brewery & Pub.

On a winter afternoon, order a beer and stand by the fire. Sip and stare at the fire. Laugh at a joke made by someone you've never met before. Sip and stare at the fire. Watch the snow fall. Sip and stare at the fire. Glance up every now and then to see the snow getting deeper. Sip and stare at the fire.

That's exactly the kind of experience owner Lark Ludlow was going for when she and her brother Barrett designed Tahquamenon Falls Brewery & Pub. They wanted a place that would combine the beautiful scenery of the northern Michigan woods with good food and beer to create an experience like no other. And they wanted to do it in a way that their grandfather, John Barrett, would appreciate.

The land now occupied by the entrance to the state park, the parking lot, and the brewpub once belonged to Barrett. He was a lumberman who bought 164 acres of northern Michigan woods around the famous falls with plans to establish a logging camp. But when Barrett learned that the state was acquiring land for a park, he donated all but two acres of his property to the state.

Graced with an outdoor fireplace that always has a roaring fire, Tahquamenon Falls Brewery & Pub might be the best brewery to visit in the middle of winter.

Barrett appreciated the need to preserve the area around the falls, but he was also a businessman. In talks with the state, he negotiated a deed restriction that mandated the road and parking lot would end three-quarters of a mile from the falls, leaving the falls accessible only by foot. Those two acres he kept would be contiguous to the parking lot so he could build lumber camp–style buildings from which to sell food and souvenirs to tourists. Barrett reasoned that the falls were so remote that people who came to see them would be in need of a drink and a meal after a long drive and hike. Barrett built a large outdoor fireplace, a feature of every lumber camp, to serve as the focal point.

The concessions operated until 1987, when Ludlow and her brother, Barrett, acquired the property. The initial plan was for Barrett to quit his job as a meteorologist to run the concessions while Lark continued her work as a human resources professional in Ithaca, New York. But when they got their first look at the property, they were shocked to find the buildings were beyond repair. Nobody had maintained them over the years, and water had seeped in, rotting the wooden structures. The best option was to tear them down and start over. On the spot of the old camp, they built new lumber camp–style structures for concessions. And, in a nod to their grandfather, they built a large fireplace.

In the mid-1990s, Lark left her job and came to Michigan to help her brother run the concession stand. Soon the two began to think about other ways they could serve the park's visitors, eventually deciding that a brewpub would be a great addition that would allow them to stay open year-round. Lark would take on brewing responsibilities while Barrett continued to run the concessions.

The siblings designed the brewpub to be upscale rustic. They chose a green and brownish-red color scheme for the interior to bring in elements that reflect the outdoors and the lumber industry. They painted the chairs the same red tone as the iron ore boats that ply Lake Superior a few miles to the north. They built the footrest at the bar out of a piece of salvaged railroad track from a twenty-five-mile dead-straight stretch between Seney and Singleton. The fireplace was built with local stone, and they mounted animal skins and deer and moose heads on the wall.

The result? Lark and Barrett never dreamed they would be so successful. People come for the falls and stay for the beer. "I love it when people walk in the door and say, 'Wow!'" Lark comments.

Summer brings visitors from all over the world, and the deck is packed with people who sometimes have to wait more than an hour to be seated. Winter brings the most repeat customers—mostly people from the Lower Peninsula, Ohio, Indiana, or Wisconsin who come to snowshoe, cross-country ski, or ride the trails on snowmobiles. (The brewery and pub are open year-round, although they do close for a few weeks in the fall and spring.)

Tahquamenon Falls Brewery & Pub owner Lark Ludlow.

Despite the brewery's success, there's a note of regret in Ludlow's voice when she talks about her grandfather. She knows this brewery would not be here without his vision, and she wishes he had lived long enough to see what his grandchildren have accomplished. Ludlow says he would have appreciated the way the restaurant, gift shop, and covered deck work in harmony with the beautiful forest he helped preserve.

"Besides," Ludlow says, "he enjoyed a good beer."

THE OLD MILL BREWPUB & GRILL

717 East Bridge Street
Plainwell
269-204-6601
Oldmillbrew.com

OWNER: Scott Zylstra
BREWER: Brian Lonberg
FLAGSHIP BEERS: Crazy Beaver Cream Ale, named after a mountain bike trail at Fort Custer in Battle Creek; Island City IPA, a gateway beer for the Budweiser drinker; Plainwell Pale Ale; Railside Red; Buckwheat Brown

From the minute Scott Zylstra walked into the old J. F. Eesley Milling Company's flour mill in Plainwell, he was sold. He knew this was the place for his new brewpub. "I literally took ten steps in the room and looked at the ceiling and went, 'This is the coolest thing I have ever seen.'"

What he saw were fourteen grain chutes descending from the ceiling like wooden stalactites. But what he envisioned was a brewpub that would be different from every other brewpub in the state.

Now, some of Michigan's breweries are in old fire stations or churches. Some are in old retail businesses. Others are in new buildings constructed from the ground up, looking like they came right out of a build-it-yourself brewpub catalog. None of those places can match the charm and warmth and history of the Old Mill Brewpub & Grill in this incredible 150-year-old building that is on the National Register of Historic Places.

Where customers now sit and eat and drink, mill employees once toiled, filling bags with flour and grain that dropped down from the bins built into the floor above. Each chute was made from wooden

OLD MILL OWNER SCOTT ZYLSTRA.

Grain chutes hang down from the ceiling at the Old Mill Brewpub & Grill in Plainwell. The brewpub is in an old flour mill that's more than 150 years old.

Trains regularly rumble past the window of the Old Mill, almost close enough to touch.

planks that were constructed to form a four-sided funnel. The bins that held the grain are gone, but the chutes remain, a reminder of this building's previous life and the town's agricultural heritage.

The mill, built in 1870, was at one point the biggest buckwheat flour mill in the country. Over the years, the mill morphed into a small-town feed store. After the feed store closed in the mid-1990s, various small businesses moved in, including a coffee shop, flower shop, and rental hall.

No matter the tenant, the hulking building with the corrugated steel exterior remained a landmark, and it still holds a special place in the hearts of the people in Plainwell. Now that the building hosts a brewpub honoring the city's heritage, Zylstra says that people occasionally stop by to offer mementos and historical items that were generated by the mill. Shortly after opening, a town resident dropped off an old flour sack. Then a few weeks later a man brought a hundred-year-old buckwheat flour sack that he had found in an antique store. Those items are now framed and hanging on the walls.

Zylstra is proud of what he's done to breathe new life into this old building and is excited to share its charm with customers. And those customers often walk in with eyes wide with curiosity and awe. Angie Galovan, the general manager, says the first thing customers usually ask about is the building's history. The next thing they ask is, what's the deal with the ceiling?

"Once we get people to Old Mill, they are sold," Galovan says. Just like its owner was.

SALT SPRINGS BREWERY

117 South Ann Arbor Street
Saline
734-295-9191
Saltspringsbrewery.com

OWNERS: Ron Schofield and Mark Zadvinskis
BREWER: Ed Borsius
FLAGSHIP BEERS: Big Brown Bunny, an English porter; Boreal Forest, an American IPA; Crispy's Tipple; Heavenly Hefeweizen; Kick Axe Kölsch

When Ron Schofield moved to Saline in 1990, one building immediately caught his eye: the church at the corner of Ann Arbor Street and East Henry Street. It was unlike anything else in this small town south of Ann Arbor. It was love at first sight.

The building, constructed in 1899, dominates the corner and the neighborhood. Its stone foundation, crenellated wall, and arches make the church look like a castle, and the brick steeple looks like the sentry tower of a fort. It is charming and intimidating at the same time, Schofield thought, and it would be a great place for a brewery.

Schofield had toyed with the idea of opening a brewery for twenty years—he even discussed it with his friend Ed Borsius, a home brewer. But he just couldn't bring himself to think of it as a realistic goal. Finally, urged on by family and friends, Schofield began to seriously consider the opportunity, and he and Borsius looked at possible locations in and around Saline. Problem was, they didn't see anything that excited them. The location of Schofield's dreams wasn't available. Even though the congregation moved to a new facility in 1990, the old church was occupied by a succession of businesses—a book and gift shop, a coffee shop and children's

The ceiling at Salt Springs Brewery has been painted with a mural intended to evoke Michelangelo's *The Creation of Adam* on the ceiling of the Sistine Chapel in Vatican City.

Salt Springs brewer Ed Borsius.

play space, and finally a rental hall for parties and wedding receptions.

What Schofield didn't know was that there was someone else in the area who also coveted the old church as a space for a brewery. That, surprisingly enough, was his neighbor, Mark Zadvinskis, who had moved to Saline from Ann Arbor just a couple of years earlier. One day in conversation, the two discovered they shared an interest in beer and a mutual love for a certain building. In fact, Zadvinskis had looked into buying the old church years earlier, but didn't because the timing just wasn't right.

Zadvinskis, Schofield, and Borsius decided to cast their lot together but agreed they would wait until they found the right place in or near downtown Saline. They did not want their brewery to be a storefront in a strip mall. They wanted to be a bigger part of the community, and the perfect place, they all agreed, would be the old church.

Then came the day when their real estate agent said the owners of the old church were thinking about retiring. Rather than wait for the building to come on the market, the three approached the owners with an offer. Time was of the essence because Zadvinskis, Schofield, and Borsius knew that other entrepreneurs were also nosing around town for space to open a brewery. If they hesitated for even a second it would be too late.

Once the papers were signed, the new owners spent five months on renovations. They put the kitchen in the old choir room, reinforced the old organ loft for seating, removed and replaced part of the floor with a concrete slab to support the fermenters, and overhauled sewers and water lines to meet the needs of the brewhouse in the basement.

Meanwhile, an eager community followed their progress through the newspaper and social media. People who walked in to check on the status of the brewpub often volunteered their services as laborers. And when a local painting company heard about the renovation, the owners donated their services just to be a part of the project.

The result was a beautiful brewpub. Stained glass windows on the south and west side filter the sunlight entering the pub and bathe the interior in pastels. The walls gently curve into the ceiling, and in the center of that ceiling is a painting of a hand with an extended index finger reaching or pointing to hops cones on a vine. The image is intended to evoke Michelangelo's *The Creation of Adam* on the ceiling of the Sistine Chapel in Vatican City.

That description may make it sound as if Schofield and Zadvinskis are being irreverent, but the opposite would be true. The mural is intended to pay respect to the former church, life itself, and the creation of beer. The owners take pains to make sure that they are not being disrespectful to the former place of worship. They temper their pride with humility because they know that this building is special to people in the community; they frequently hear from customers who were baptized, married or used to worship in this space.

"Everybody working on the renovation gave a little bit more because they knew what this building was, what it was going to be, and what it meant to the community," Schofield says.

Patience, it seems, has its virtues.

ELK STREET BREWERY AND TAPROOM

ELK STREET BREWERY AND TAPROOM

3 South Elk Street
Sandusky
810-648-1600
Elkstreetbrewery.com

OWNERS: Ron and Anne Hasenbusch
BREWER: Ron Hasenbusch
FLAGSHIP BEERS: Crimson Elk IPA; Amber Wave; Sandusky Session, a lower-alcohol gateway beer

This is a story about Anne and Ron Hasenbusch, who decided to toss aside their comfortable life in Grosse Pointe to pursue their dream and follow their passion for beer.

Full disclosure: Ron and Anne are former neighbors of mine. One of their sons was in the same grade as one of my daughters during elementary and middle school. I didn't know them particularly well, but I knew they were nice people. I knew Anne did some substitute teaching in the area, and I knew Ron as a quiet metallurgical engineer for Ford Motor Company. I also knew that they were good parents who always attended important school events. But during our children's high school years it was like they disappeared; I never saw them around.

That is, until one day when I ran into Anne in a grocery store. When I stopped to chat, she unloaded about how she and Ron were building a house and moving to the Thumb because her husband had a crazy idea to buy a farm to *grow hops*.

Crazy? Not at all, I assured her. Ron wasn't crazy; he was a visionary. With craft beer exploding and the demand for hops growing, his timing was perfect.

She seemed to be put at ease by my assurances, but it was easy

ELK STREET BREWERY CO-OWNERS RON AND ANNE HASENBUSCH.

The Elk Street Brewery occupies an old building on busy intersection in Sandusky, a small farm town in the Thumb.

to tell that she was still worried. And then I heard nothing more about them for two more years until the "aha" moment happened. I was chatting with friends about writing this book, and one said I should get in touch with Anne and Ron—she'd seen on Facebook that they were opening a brewery in Sandusky.

Good for them! Opening a brewery seemed like a logical next step after investing in a hops farm, but . . . Sandusky? Could they really make this work in an agricultural town with a population of fewer than three thousand?

Well, not only are Anne and Ron making it work, the Elk Street Brewery and Taproom has been so successful that they needed to expand after only two years in business.

The cozy brewery and restaurant at the corner of Elk Street and Sanilac Road is unlike anything else for miles around. Of course it's in one of those classic late nineteenth-century brick buildings with oak floors and pressed-tin ceilings that populate towns across Michigan. But stepping into the Elk Street Brewery and Taproom feels like you are entering one of those "trendy spots." Mounted heads and elk antlers dominate the walls, but its selection of beer and a foodie-like menu items (elk siders!) make it feel more like a place you might find in Ferndale, Grand Rapids, or Traverse City.

Yet Elk Street Brewery is a come-as-you-are place; Ron and Anne have hosted big family dinners featuring people in formal evening wear while others have come through the door in their dirty jeans and work boots, straight off the tractor.

And that to me is the coolest thing about Elk Street Brewery. It redefines small-town life without losing its small-town feel. It's a place to get good beer and food that's a cut above average but it doesn't make you feel like somehow you are not worthy or urbane or hip enough.

Owning a brewery has been one of Anne and Ron's dreams for more than thirty years. They started talking about it in 1984 after Anne gave Ron a home brewing kit for his birthday when they were students at Western Michigan University. A few years later, Ron wrote a business plan for an imaginary brewery for an assignment while working on a master's degree in business at Central Michigan University. The two talked about opening a brewery every so often throughout their married lives, but with a young family and growing careers the time never seemed right.

In 2011, the couple took the first step when Ron bought the two-and-a-half acre farm to grow hops. The plan was to sell most of the harvest but put some aside for Ron's home brewing hobby. About the same time, Anne decided it was time for a career change; teaching just wasn't for her anymore. So the family left Grosse Pointe to start a new life in the Thumb—kind of. Ron continued to work at his job at a Ford Motor Company plant in Livonia, tending to the farm on weekends.

Once they settled into their new home in Port Sanilac, Ron's home brewing hobby became more than a hobby. First, he built a shed for his brewing equipment, then moved everything to the larger space of the garage when that was finished. ("We couldn't even park cars in there," Anne laughs.)

Ron was now brewing small batches every other weekend, but what they did not realize was that he was ramping up to something bigger. With both Anne and Ron about to turn fifty, they decided it was time to take stock; if they were going to do this brewery thing—if they were going to finally reach for their dream—they would have to do it now or stop talking about it. After a short search they knew they had the right location when they found the building in Sandusky. It was at a busy corner near the county courthouse and a community park. Over the years, the building had housed a combination pool hall and grocery store, archery range, milliner's, barber supply shop, arcade, accountant's office, cell phone store, and mortgage lender. In addition to the good location, Anne and Ron say, the building spoke to them; it was a once-proud structure, full of character and warmth, and it was calling out to them for a new life.

The brewery has been busy since the doors opened in November

Elk Street Brewery co-owner and brewer Ron Hasenbusch uses a refractometer to check the gravity of his wort.

2014. In fact, it's so popular that Ron and Anne decided to expand into the building that used to house a fitness gym next door. The brewery will now have two sides connected by a doorway in the middle. The new space will be a place for beer, conversation, cornhole, darts, and American shuffleboard. One wall will be exposed brick and the ceiling will be made from old pallets. When the expansion is complete, they will finally have a space they can rent out for private parties and wedding receptions.

After they've accomplished this, Ron figures he'll throttle back a little bit. He plans to continue to work at Ford in Livonia and brew on the weekends until retirement. Surprisingly, the brewery has given Anne a chance to return to teaching. Her subject now, however, is Beer 101. She's taken on the role of the brewery's chief beer evangelist, educating people on different beer styles and how hops impact a beer's flavor. She's getting great satisfaction from seeing people who used to drink only the beers with the lowest IBUs move up to hoppier beers.

But the best thing about running a brewery, they say, is the feeling they get when people come in to this small-town pub and are surprised by the quality of the beer—beer they might suppose is only available from breweries in larger, hipper, more sophisticated cities.

For any brewer, that's a dream come true.

➤➤➤➤➤

ONE MORE THING: If you need a reason to go to the Elk Street Brewery and Taproom, try going to Sandusky for Thumb Festival, a typical small-town gala held annually in the third week in June. In the winter, go for the Country Christmas Parade on the first weekend of December when all the area farmers decorate their tractors with lights and drive them through town. And if you see Anne and Ron, please tell them I said hi and send my best wishes.

ORE DOCK BREWING COMPANY

114 Spring Street
Marquette
906-228-8888
Ore-Dock.com

OWNERS: Andrea and Weston Pernsteiner
BREWER: Nick Vancourt
FLAGSHIP BEERS: Reclamation IPA; Saison, an ale brewed with malt from France and a single hop; Bum's Beach Wheat, an American-style wheat beer with Mount Hood and Fuggles hops

There are lots of places where people can meet for important gatherings, study sessions, or special events—coffee shops, libraries, banquet halls. In Marquette, however, people have an additional option, the Ore Dock (named for this Lake Superior port city's two iconic ore docks). This venue just happens to make beer.

Walk into the Ore Dock Brewing Company's taproom and you might wonder what the big deal is. The taproom is a long, relatively narrow space that leads back to the brewhouse behind a glass wall. It has a nice feel to it; the walls are plastered with announcements for upcoming concerts and bike races and the like, and there are lots of conversations going on, but it's a bit more like a sports bar than a community space.

But go back out the door, walk up the stairs to the second floor, turn right, and the lightbulb goes on. This is the room that owners Wes and Andrea Pernsteiner call the Community Space. It's a room with exposed sandstone walls, exposed wooden beams, south-facing windows, cozy leather chairs in one corner, booths along one wall, and a concert stage. It's a place where people can come to study, chat, and hold meetings. It's also a place where people can attend

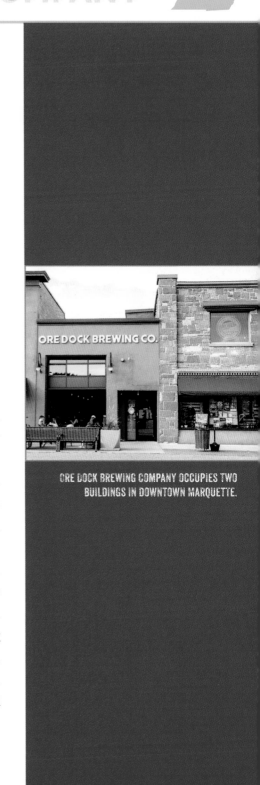

ORE DOCK BREWING COMPANY OCCUPIES TWO BUILDINGS IN DOWNTOWN MARQUETTE.

lectures, concerts, plays, and family gatherings and celebrations.

In short, this is where Marquette comes together.

Visit the Community Space on a weekday afternoon and you might find students from nearby Northern Michigan University in a cram session or working on a group project. In the evening, one part of the room may be taken over by a professor giving a free science lecture. Or on a weekend evening, you might catch a performance by a bluegrass or blues band or a standup comedian. Or maybe you'll find a fashion show, a reception for the opening of an art exhibit, or a production of a Shakespearian play. On a Saturday afternoon, the space could host a wedding reception or two, and on a Sunday it could be a baby shower.

As often and as variously as the space is rented, it is never closed off entirely. Even if one side is rented for a baby shower or a wedding reception, the other side of the room remains open for people to study or chat.

⋙

It's only appropriate that the best-selling beer at Ore Dock Brewing Company is called Reclamation IPA because both the building that houses the Community Space and the city of Marquette are successful reclamation projects. The Pernsteiners reclaimed the building after years of neglect. Marquette, meanwhile, has emerged from decades of economic struggle to become the Upper Peninsula's most dynamic city. Today, Marquette has a vibe that makes this town of twenty-one thousand people feel much larger.

The two-story structure that houses Ore Dock today was built in the 1860s from sandstone mined in the area. Over the years, the building housed various businesses, but when brewery owners Wes and Andrea Pernsteiner bought it, it had most recently held a transmission repair shop on the first floor and a vehicle storage garage on the second floor, with a ramp connecting the two. When the thirty or so cars on the second floor were removed, the Persteiners realized they had a huge job on their hands. They sandblasted the walls to remove the whitewash. They bought old booths from a closed restaurant and reupholstered them with old blankets from an army surplus store. They built tables with wood

Trains regularly rumble past the window of the Old Mill, almost close enough to touch.

that had at one time been the floor of an old sawmill. Then they had a local artist come in to seal the wooden floor—still stained with tire treads and burn marks from welding torches—and build a fireplace. Then the ramp was removed, the hole in the floor filled, and new bathrooms and a bar built in that space. Once it was completed, the brewery received beautification and historical preservation awards from the city.

During the afternoons, the Ore Dock's Community Space is popular with students from Northern Michigan University. On evenings and weekends, the space is used for everything from concerts to wedding showers and receptions to lectures and meetings.

Since opening, the Community Space has been in constant use. But there seems to be something mystical about this old auto dealership with sandsone walls that attracts members of the Northern Michigan University history faculty. Faculty members give monthly public lectures in the Community Space and kind of just hang around other times. Those regular visits from the university's history faculty inspired a unique collaboration: head brewer Nick Vancourt made a special beer (a gruit, an ancient beer bittered with herbs rather than hops) for an event the brewery held in conjunction with the university's history department to celebrate the proper burial of England's King Richard III in March 2015. The beer's name: Final Coronation. Vancourt has also worked with the university to make Sahti beer, a traditional Finnish ale that is flavored with juniper berries instead of hops.

There are two other unusual aspects of the Ore Dock. First, even though it has two bars, the one on the upper floor is staffed only for an event. So if you want a beer, stop in the taproom before going upstairs. Second, people often wander in off the street just to look around. Sometimes they are sizing the room up for a future rental, other times they come in just because they've heard about it. "I hear all the time from people who say, 'My god, it's so cool up there,'" Pernsteiner says. "From the front door you can't tell what's up there."

Maybe you can't, but it's likely to be busy.

REDWOOD STEAKHOUSE AND BREWERY

5304 Gateway Centre Drive
Flint
810-233-8000
Redwoodbrewingco.com

GENERAL MANAGER: Luis Fernandes
BREWER: Konrad Connor
FLAGSHIP BEERS: Light and Kölsch; Munich Helles; English Pale; Brown Porter; Cream Stout; American IPA

Unless you live in the Flint area or regularly drive on U.S. 23 south of the interchange with I-75, you've probably never heard of the Redwood Steakhouse and Brewery. Surprisingly, its high-profile location right off the freeway doesn't seem to raise the level of awareness that it exists. People who pass it on the highway are usually focused on getting somewhere else. Besides, most people just can't imagine that there can be a good brewery at the end of a dead-end street in an office park.

But you should not dismiss Redwood based simply on its lack of name recognition. Get off U.S. 23 and weave your way through the streets and you will be surprised by Redwood Steakhouse and Brewery. Adorned with log walls, beams, and pillars, and featuring a stone fireplace, it resembles a classic northern California lodge. And when you look up at those grand wooden beams, you will see banners proclaiming this little-known brewery's accomplishments:

GREAT AMERICAN BEER FESTIVAL

2012: Silver medal, *Coffee Beer Category*—Hazelnut Coffee Cream Stout

2011: Silver medal, *Sweet Stout Category*—Cream Stout

2009: Silver medal, *Sweet Stout Category*—Cream Stout

2008: Great American Beer Festival Small Brewpub of the Year

2008: Gold medal, *Sweet Stout Category*—Cream Stout

2008: Gold medal, *European Style Dunkel Category*—Dunkel

2005: Bronze medal, *American Dark Lager Category*—Darth's Dark Lager

2003: Gold medal, *British Stout Category*—Cream Stout

2002: Silver medal, *Sweet Stout Category*—Cream Stout

WORLD BEER CUP

2014: Bronze award, Sweet or Cream Stout Category—Cream Stout

2010: Silver award, *Sweet Stout Category*—Cream Stout

2008: Bronze award, *English Style Mild Ale Category*—The Mild One

2006: Bronze award, *Sweet Stout Category*—Cream Stout

2004: Gold award, *Belgian Style Saison Category*—Saison Redwood

2004: Bronze award, *Sezoens (Belgian Other Style) Category*—Belgian Brown Ale

2002: Gold award, *Old Ale Category*—Old English Ale

2002: Bronze award, *Sweet Stout Category*—Cream Stout

Michigan has bigger breweries and better-known breweries, but Redwood is the little brewery that could.

Redwood's direction was set by legendary Michigan brewer Bill Wamby when he arrived from the now-defunct Big Buck Brewery in Auburn Hills in the early 2000s. Wamby turned Redwood into a brewing powerhouse by focusing on traditional English-, German-, and Czech-style beers and immediately improved the quality of the beer by doing something simple but often overlooked: making sure the brewing equipment was consistently clean and sanitized. From there, it was just a matter of fine-tuning the recipes to brew consistently good beers that met style guidelines.

Surprisingly, Wamby did not set out to make Redwood one of the state's most celebrated breweries. Wamby says he entered Redwood's beers in contests like the World Beer Cup because he just wanted to see how his beer stacked up next to the big, established brewers. "A lot of people think it's an ego thing. That's not true," Wamby says. "We didn't get anything for it—no recognition or pay. But it helped you mentally because it gave you a challenge."

Today, Konrad Connor carries on Redwood's brewing traditions. Connor had been a home brewer and a member of Redwood's Mug Club who would raise his hand and volunteer to help clean up the brewery or package beer in exchange for a growler. Then came the Friday when Connor learned that his job as a computer programmer had been outsourced. He left his former place of business in the late morning and headed immediately for Redwood for a beer and to think about what would come next. Before he left, Wamby offered Connor a part-time job.

On his first day in his new job, Connor recalls, Wamby provided a crash course in sanitation and chemistry and instilled in Connor a complete understanding of the brewing process and the importance of attention to detail. "When I started here I didn't know anything," Connor says. "All the basics came from Bill."

Connor says his brewing philosophy comes straight from Wamby: if you want to cut corners, you should just quit because you are on the wrong path.

Over the years, Wamby has instilled those same traits in his other assistants: Adam Beratta, who brews at Axle Brewing Company in Ferndale, and David Shaw, who went on to brew at Parker's Hilltop Brewery in Clarkston.

"I want to make the highest-quality beer I can," Connor says. "Bill set the bar and it's pretty darned hard to stay there. I think that's why so many of his people have gone on to success. He set the high standard."

Still, you don't have to take Connor's word for it. Next time you are near Flint, don't drive past. Instead, stop in, order a beer, and look up at the banners.

4

COLLABEERATION

Russell Springsteen of Right Brain Brewing remembers it as a real uh-oh moment.

It was shortly after Right Brain had opened, and he and some of the guys at Dark Horse Brewing were brewing a beer together at Right Brain's Traverse City brewhouse. Springsteen was preparing to pitch yeast into the wort when he noticed the Dark Horse guys looking uneasy. Springsteen noted the sideways glances and murmurs, but didn't know why.

The following week, Springsteen and some of his brewers made the journey down to Dark Horse's brewery in Marshall to complete the collaboration brew. As a courtesy, Springsteen brought a couple of growlers of his beer to share. When none of the Dark Horse guys would touch his beer, he knew something was up.

That's when Dark Horse owner Aaron Morse spoke up. He told Springsteen in a polite but firm tone that Springsteen would have to change the way he was handling yeast. Morse had seen Springsteen move yeast from one fermenter to another without bothering to see if there were enough or checking whether the yeast was healthy enough to go into a new batch. Morse was clear: if Springsteen was going to make Michigan beer, he was going to make *great* Michigan beer. If Right Brain was going to produce bad beer, it would reflect poorly on all the state's other brewers.

The next day, Springsteen went back to his Traverse City brewery and overhauled his operations.

Springsteen is thankful for Morse's admonition. Morse didn't have to point out the problem with his brewing technique. If Right Brain failed because its beer was bad, what difference would it make to the Dark Horse guys?

Brewers everywhere—even among the nation's biggest and most competitive breweries—are a brotherhood. When they're together,

> BREWERIES ARE FUN PLACES TO HANG AROUND. THEY ARE FULL OF PEOPLE WHO CARE ABOUT WHAT THEY DO AND HAVE FUN DOING IT.
> —MIKE EME, BREWER, CHEBOYGAN BREWING COMPANY

all they talk about is brewing and beer—the how-tos and the what-ifs; do this, don't do that, and try this—and they are happily willing to leave it to the marketing side to fight it out for grocery store shelf space and tavern tap handles.

Rather than being competitors, brewers in Michigan see themselves largely as collaborators on a common project: producing great Michigan beer. That sense of pride and collaboration was established in the early 1990s when there were just a few brewers in the state. True, there was some initial animosity toward one another, but they soon realized that if they wanted to survive they needed to collaborate, share knowledge, and help one another when times were tough.

It's a spirit one might call *collabeeration*. It's a spirit that allows a brewer to pick up the phone and call another brewer down the street or across the state to ask for the brewing equivalent of a cup of sugar. It's gives small brewers and start-ups the ability to tap the knowledge and expertise of the state's most experienced brewers. It's also a spirit that imposes a sense of responsibility on the established brewers to act as mentors to the state's neophytes.

"There's a community of breweries and we have a responsibility to help each other," says Dave Engbers, one of the owners of Founders Brewing Company in Grand Rapids. "I think as one of the older breweries, I'm hoping that we influence these younger breweries to really hone their craft and become better brewers."

Brewing today has a do-it-yourself and use-your-own-imagination ethic. Brewers can do all the basic stuff of their enterprises: wire a boiler, design a label, run a forklift, manage the books, and run to the bank to deposit the receipts. They're proud and independent entrepreneurs. But among brewers there's also a desire to collaborate on issues important to the industry: figure out ways to use less water, encourage local farmers to grow ingredients, foster the growth and success of young brewers, and help more women break into this male-dominated industry.

The spirit of collabeeration was born in the mid-1990s, according to Rex Halfpenny, publisher of the *Michigan Beer Guide*. The few brewers in the state all viewed each other cautiously, from a distance—so insecure about what they were doing that they refused even to go into each other's breweries. Realizing that the brewers shared one vital thing concern—they all wanted to sell more beer—Halfpenny saw an opening. He quickly formed the Michigan Brewers Guild, basing it on the brewers guild model he saw working in Oregon. Soon Michigan's brewers were holding monthly meetings to figure out ways to promote their beer. They quickly discovered they had plenty in common: similar problems with equipment and technology, sourcing ingredients, and distribution. Before long, the animosity that cleaved them morphed into the cooperation that bound them.

Once that breakthrough occurred, a real spirit of unity arose among Michigan brewers, says Tim Selewski, general manager at Royal Oak Brewery, which opened in 1995. "There's unity now, but there was a different kind of unity when there were only thirty breweries in the state. You really all pulled the rope together."

Bill Wrobel, one of the owners of Dragonmead in Warren, says he continues to be amazed by the generosity of the Michigan beer community. He would have no qualms calling anybody in the state to say that he needed to borrow a bag of grain because he knows the response he would get: when do you want us to bring it to you?

Even before the doors opened at Batch Brewing Company in Detroit, owners Stephen Roginson and Jason Williams were depending on the kindness of other brewers. Shortly after the brewery opening was announced, they got a call from Scott Sullivan, one of the owners of Greenbush Brewing Company (more than two hundred miles away in southwestern Michigan), offering to do a collaboration brew. Atwater Brewery let them use its equipment to keg their beer, Motor City Brewing Works lent them its keg washers before their equipment was installed, and Bret and Eric Kuhnhenn helped with technical support on how to set up and run the brewery.

Mark Rieth of Atwater Brewery says his willingness to help the Batch guys proceeded equally from altruism and self-interest. "The better the industry does as a whole, the better you're going to do as a brewery."

I saw the spirit of collabeeration in action when I was interviewing

Duncan Williams, the brewer at Grizzly Peak in Ann Arbor. We were sitting in the taproom when Chris Davies, head brewer at Arbor Brewing Company—just a few blocks down the street—came through the door. Williams knew exactly what Davies had come for and after exchanging pleasantries Williams dashed off to the brewhouse and returned with an eleven-pound box of Cascade hops in exchange for receiving an emergency loan of hops a week earlier. Davies stuck around for a beer, and he and Williams talked about what was on their respective brewing schedules and what supplies they might need and might be able to share. The hop exchange between Williams and Davies is the kind of transaction that happens hundreds of times a year among Michigan's brewers and is representative of how the brewers relate to and respect one another.

That's not to say everyone in the Michigan brewing community stands around the campfire holding hands and singing "Kumbaya." Longtime brewers say that some of that sense of camaraderie is starting to fray. There are so many brewers in the state now that it's just not possible for everybody to know everybody else, which makes it harder to build the same level of rapport. Consider: in 2016, Original Gravity Brewing Company of Milan sued Final Gravity Brewing Company of Decatur for trademark infringement. In federal court, the owners of Original Gravity argued that Final Gravity's name caused confusion among consumers who might purchase Final Gravity's products thinking they had purchased something from Original Gravity. A few days later, however, the lawsuit was dropped after the owners of the two breweries talked, had a beer together, and worked things out.

Given the number of breweries that are opening statewide and nationwide, it seems likely that this kind of conflict is likely to arise more often in the future. Still, litigation is frowned upon in the community and most breweries would prefer to work things out with a handshake.

Duncan Williams of Grizzly Peak says disputes in the craft brewing industry are usually resolved without going to court because, he says, "The industry is 98 percent asshole free." John Linardos of Motor City Brewing Works echoes that sentiment, saying brewers prefer imagination and creativity over competition and confrontation. "The minute you start to compete, it's no longer rewarding. If you ever get the urge to compete, remember why you wanted to do this in the beginning."

At Right Brain, owner Russell Springsteen believes competition can be a good thing when it's fostered the right way. People who are thinking about staring their own brewery regularly ask Springsteen for advice, and he gives it gladly. He'll open the books to show the new brewers how his company operates, manages money, and handles purchasing. "It creates a more educated competition," Springsteen says. "We do compete with one another—for sure we do. We're trying to make better beer than the next guy. But if they're making it better, then I better get better."

DARK HORSE BREWING COMPANY

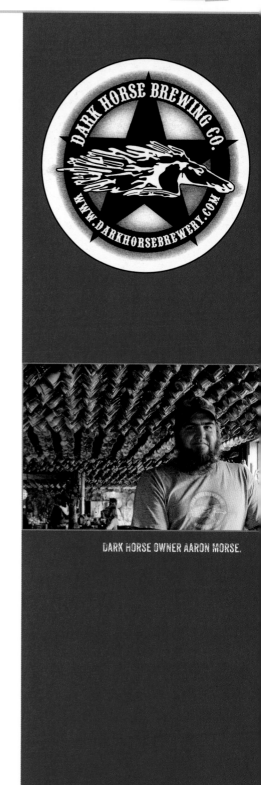

DARK HORSE OWNER AARON MORSE.

511 South Kalamazoo Avenue
Marshall
269-781-9940
Darkhorsebrewery.com

OWNER: Aaron Morse
FLAGSHIP BEERS: Crooked Tree IPA, the brewery's best-selling beer; Raspberry Ale; Black Ale, a good-drinking, malty dark beer that doesn't fall into a style category; Boffo Brown Ale

There's a sign taped to the jukebox in the taproom at Dark Horse Brewing Company:

DO NOT PLAY AC/DC ON THIS JUKEBOX. YOUR SONG WILL BE SKIPPED. NO REFUNDS

You're in Aaron Morse's taproom, dammit, and don't you forget it. The sign might make Morse sound like a jerk or a bully, but he's not. He's polite, generous, and smart. By his own account, he's a momma's boy. But the jukebox sign reflects Morse's approach to life and brewing: have fun, do things the right way, and don't put up with any bullshit.

AC/DC is bullshit, says Morse. So is Nickelback, the Canadian rock band. Representatives from Nickelback called Morse a few years ago. Seeking karma, the band members asked if they could use Dark Horse's beer and logo to make a music video to support their 2008 album, *Dark Horse*. Morse would have been entirely justified in rejecting the proposal because the concept didn't match with the brewery's goals, but he rejected Nickelback for another reason. "I told them no because their music sucks," Morse says with a sly smile.

Morse's approach to brewing is just as passionate and uncompromising. He expects to produce beers of the highest quality

and he expects every other brewer in the state to do the same.

Brewers are constantly in and out of each other's breweries and sharing beers with each other, so Morse gets to see and taste what's going on all over the state. He knows there are a hundred different ways to brew beer, and he doesn't claim to be a beer oracle. But when he sees practices in other breweries that are questionable, he speaks up. But he'll treat you better than he did the guys in Nickleback; his is *constructive* criticism, whether it's about cleaning practices, the handling of ingredients, or equipment.

Why should Morse care what other brewers are doing? Because he believes that if one craft brewer is producing bad beer, it reflects poorly on all the other craft brewers in the state, and that puts his brewery—his very livelihood—at stake. Therefore, Morse wants to make sure that all brewers, especially the new guys, do some simple things to ensure the quality of their product. First and foremost, he wants to help new brewers understand the importance of cleaning their equipment properly. Many of the new guys coming into the business in the past few years developed their chops as home brewers, and the level of cleanliness that they're used to just isn't good enough for a larger-scale operation. Second, Morse wants to make sure brewers aren't using stale or poor ingredients. Finally, Morse stresses continuing education. He doesn't care if you went to brewing school or learned how to brew as an apprentice or out of a book. Every brewer needs to continue to learn and grow.

❯❯❯❯❯

The Dark Horse Brewery is more than just a brewhouse and a taproom. On the grounds of the brewery there's a tattoo parlor; candy store; motorcycle parts store; a general store that sells beer, home brewing supplies, maple syrup, skateboards, and Dark Horse clothing; a hair salon; a coffee roaster; and Morse's other company, which does spray foam insulation. Morse says the variety reflects his eclectic personality and varied interests.

Morse graduated from Northern Michigan University with an art degree, and he and his wife, Kristine, built the Dark Horse taproom with their own hands. More than anything else, Morse wants the taproom to be a place where locals and beer tourists can meet and mingle and maybe even let rip a little bit. Morse allows patrons to scratch their names into the taproom's tables and walls, and he encourages customers to put stickers and art on the taproom's ceilings and walls.

"The only thing we take serious around here is the beer," Morse says. "It's our livelihood and it's important to us."

Aaron Morse wants his customers to feel comfortable in Dark Horse's taproom so he allows them to carve their names into the wooden tables and walls and leave behind artwork and mementos.

KUHNHENN BREWING COMPANY

5919 Chicago Road
Warren
586-979-8361

36000 Groesbeck Highway
Clinton Township
586-231-0249

Kbrewery.com

OWNERS: Eric Kuhnhenn, Bret Kuhnhenn, and Julijana Kuhnhenn
HEAD BREWER: Paul Brady
FLAGSHIP BEERS: DRIPA, a double rice IPA that won the gold medal at the 2012 World Beer Cup for American-style India Pale Ale; Loonie Kuhnie Pale Ale; the Fluffer, a session IPA; Simcoe Silly, an American-Belgian-style strong ale brewed with Belgian yeast and Simcoe hops

Most people consume beer, but beer consumes brothers Eric and Bret Kuhnhenn, the two primary owners of Kuhnhenn Brewing Company in Warren. Beer is their life, and there is almost nothing else.

That's not to suggest that they are unhealthy in their relentless approach. They are happy, and they're just doing what other Michigan brewers are doing—building a business with an eye on growth and the future. Sitting back and saying, "That's good enough" is just not in the DNA of many brewery owners, and the Kuhnhenns are no different.

Their story starts in 1972 when their dad, Eric Kuhnhenn Sr., bought a hardware store in Warren. Both Eric and Bret started

working in their father's store in the early 1990s, which is about the same time that Eric started home brewing in his apartment at Eastern Michigan University. Bret was hooked with his first taste of his brother's brew, and quickly started his own brewing operation at their parents' house. By the time they had reached their midtwenties, both were beer fiends, brewing whatever they could with whatever ingredients they could find and seeking out different and unusual brands and varieties.

Tired of driving across southeastern Michigan to find home brewing supplies, in 1992 Eric and Bret decided to convert part of their father's hardware store into a home brewing store, starting with Bret's initial purchase of $4,000 worth of brewing supplies. Eric was onboard with the idea, but $4,000? "I thought he was crazy," Eric says, throwing his head back in mock disgust at the memory.

Initial sales were slow but began to grow after the brothers built a mailing list of customers and started producing a home brewing newsletter with recipes. As sales improved, the brothers began to think about the next step: opening their own brewery. But first, Bret decided he needed to get professional brewing experience. He worked as a bottler at the now-defunct King Brewing Company in Pontiac and brewed beer at Dragonmead on Saturdays. At both establishments, his co-workers kept asking, "When are you going to open your own place?"

In 2001, the brothers persuaded their dad to convert half the hardware store into a brewery. This time, it was their dad's turn to think that *both* of them were crazy. But Eric and Bret persuaded him, and soon he was learning three-phase electrical wiring and helping to connect the brewery's pipes and tanks. The three needed to do as much work as they could by themselves to make the project affordable. The brewery opened in 2002, but the brothers kept the hardware store open and continued to provide services like screen repair on the side to ensure they had income.

Despite their caution, it was clear early on that the brewery would be a success. Soon their half-barrel brewing system was maxed out, so Eric and Bret replaced it with a 8.5-barrel system. Of course, they installed it themselves. Needing more space, the brothers bought an adjacent auto repair shop, gutted it, and installed a four-vessel system to brew more beer every day. Of course, they did most of the work themselves. In 2005, the brothers decided the brewery and taproom needed even more space, so they blew out the wall and took what was left of the hardware store. Again, they did most of the work themselves.

Over the course of 2015 and 2016, they supplemented their operations with a full-scale production brewery and bottling plant on Groesbeck Highway in Clinton Township. Every step of the way, the brothers did as much of the work as they could to keep costs low. (On the day I visited, I found Eric rewiring the boiler.)

When they weren't wielding sledgehammers and pipe wrenches, they continued to work hard at perfecting their craft, planning time off around beer festivals and even going so far as to vacation in Belgium just to visit breweries. It was on the Belgium trip that Bret had two revelations. First, the secret to a good beer is its drinkability, even at a high level of alcohol. Good beer shouldn't be syrupy, overly heavy, or over the top in its bitterness. Second, he learned something that turned his world on its head. As a beer purist, he had always thought that using adjuncts such as rice and corn was an insult inflicted upon beer drinkers by the big industrial brewers looking to use the cheapest raw materials possible. "I was shocked by how many adjuncts the Belgians were adding to their beers," Bret says.

The trip to Belgium helped Eric and Bret sharpen their brewing philosophy. They would focus on making drinkable beers, and they now had the courage to use adjuncts to give each of their beers a distinct personality. Among the first beers they experimented with was their IPA. They discovered that adding long-grain rice to their American-style IPA gave the beer a clarity that is unusual for an IPA and a drier, less hoppy finish. They called their new concoction DRIPA, an acronym for Double Rice India Pale Ale.

Little did they know at the time that DRIPA would change the craft brewing world.

Confident that they were making good beer, the brothers decided to enter DRIPA in the 2012 World Beer Cup competition in San Diego. Much to their surprise, it was awarded the gold medal for American-style IPAs. The only problem was, *technically*, DRIPA did not meet the definition of a craft beer—at that time—because it used a rice adjunct.

DRIPA's gold medal prodded the Brewers Association to reconsider the definition of craft beer. As much as craft brewers wanted to separate themselves from the big industrial brewers, adjuncts are a natural part of beer, going back to the earliest days of brewing in North America when colonists used ingredients like spruce tips and dandelions to give their beer flavor. In 2014, the Brewers Association removed the restrictions on adjuncts.

The gold medal for DRIPA was satisfying for the Kuhnhenn brothers, but the location of the competition made the win extra sweet. "It was a big deal to win in San Diego," Eric says with a smile of satisfaction. "The Californians believe they rule all."

Almost overnight, DRIPA went from a small percentage of their sales to almost 50 percent, which brought them great satisfaction—because they did it themselves.

ONE MORE THING: The Kuhnhenn brothers are both good guys. They are gregarious and fun to be around, but at the same time they are serious and know that they can never lose focus of what got them to this point: a lot of hard work. Believe it or not, both look back fondly at the early days of the brewery when they would sleep on grain bags after making beer in the morning and working in the taproom until closing at 2 a.m. Now, they say, they are only working twelve-hour days.

Still, Bret says they are glad to be working together after all they've been through, and they are even happier they decided to move out of the hardware business. "It's way easier to sell a beer than a bolt." Bret says. "That's for sure."

GRIZZLY PEAK BREWING COMPANY

120 West Washington Street
Ann Arbor
734-741-7325
Grizzlypeak.net

OWNERS: Jon Carlson and Greg Lobdell
BREWER: Duncan Williams
FLAGSHIP BEERS: Victors Gold, a hoppy kölsch fermented with German ale yeast; Urban War Bear, a pretty aggressively hopped American-style IPA; Steelhead Red, a malt-forward beer; Bear Paw Porter, a robust American porter with lots of malt character; Shearwater IPA, which is brewed much as it would have been one hundred years ago in England

There's no hall of fame or photos hanging on the walls showcasing the young apprentices who have passed through Grizzly Peak Brewing Company in Ann Arbor on their way to becoming top-flight brewers around Michigan and across the United States. Nevertheless, the list is impressive.

Kevin Bloom, part owner of the Area 23 nano-brewery in Concord, New Hampshire, is a Grizzly Peak alumnus. Stacey Roth got her first brewing job at Grizzly Peak in 2006. She went on to work at Arbor Brewing and Arcadia Brewing Company in Battle Creek and then became production manager at Griffin Claw in Birmingham. Former Grizzly Peak brewer Jeff Hancock came to Ann Arbor while his wife was in graduate school at the University of Michigan. Once she completed her degree, they moved to back home to Washington, DC, and he's now brewer and co-owner of the district's hottest brewpub, DC Brau. Will Lawson brewed at Grizzly Peak in the late 2000s; he's now the owner and brewer at Naples Beach Brewery in Naples, Florida. Tim Schmidt was an assistant brewer for a while

DUNCAN WILLIAMS, BREWER AT GRIZZLY PEAK
BREWING COMPANY IN ANN ARBOR.

before moving to Blue Tractor and then opening Tecumseh Brewing Company. Other Grizzly Peak alumni include Oliver Roberts, who became head brewer at Wolverine State Brewing Company, and Nathan Hukill, who owns Bitter Old Fecker Rustic Ales in Chelsea. Brian Grace brewed for Grizzly Peak, too. He's now the bottling manager at Northern United Brewing Company, the production brewery in Dexter that makes everything that gets packaged for Jolly Pumpkin Artisan Ales, Grizzly Peak, and North Peak in Traverse City.

There's nothing magical about Grizzly Peak's tiny brewhouse. Working in the brewpub's claustrophobia-inducing cellar didn't provide any of those successful brewers with mystical revelations or brewing secrets. What they did get, however, was the chance to work with Duncan Williams, Grizzly Peak's head brewer. Williams's career trajectory was similar to those of many of the young people he hires today. Years ago, Ron Jeffries, then the brewer at Grizzly Peak before starting Jolly Pumpkin Artisan Ales, saw something promising in him and gave him a shot. Today, Williams is merely doing for others what Jeffries did for him.

Michigan's established brewers don't have to go out of their way to educate their protégés, but they do because it's part of the ethic. Somebody took the time and effort to teach them how to brew, so it's just right that they share their knowledge with up-and-coming brewers. Williams makes it a point to teach young brewers about the *process* of brewing through hard work and harder experience, and then he sends them on their way to continue their careers elsewhere, hoping that they will pass it on to the next generation.

Williams's story is similar to those of most other brewers of his generation. He had been a home brewer for ten years before landing his first position as a voluntary assistant at CJ's Brewing Company in Walled Lake, working with Dan Scarsella. Then he was hired as an assistant brewer at Grizzly Peak under Ron Jeffries. He learned early on that brewing has a rhythm. There's a time to mix and a time to pitch. There's a time to pump, a time to keg, and a time to clean. (Well, most of the time is spent cleaning.)

Based on what he was taught by his mentors, Williams believes the best way to teach brewing is to break each day down into simple steps. "Training begins by pointing," Williams says. "'Do this. Do that.' Or 'Let me show you how to do this, then go ahead and do it yourself. Let's look at the list of what we have to do today.' It starts off a very slow process; it's two or three weeks of just getting them used to what they need to do." He continues, "It's not necessarily me. It's the process that teaches them."

Williams's philosophy of training might seem simplistic, but it works. Stacey Roth, now of Griffin Claw, says that when training a new employee she uses what she learned from Williams at Grizzly Peak. "Duncan was really good at breaking things down," Roth says. "I appreciated the way he had things broken down in simple steps. As I try to assess the new guys coming in, I think about Duncan's structure. He had a nice schedule set up. It was very easy to base everything off time frames."

Even though schools across the state have begun to offer brewing as certificate programs and majors, Williams believes nothing beats working next to someone with many years of real-world experience. When Williams was home brewing, he bought every home brewing book he could get his hands on, but when he started working at a brewery he discovered the hard way that the theories in the books didn't always translate into the real world, and there was no substitute for learning by making mistakes.

Given so many great brewing opportunities in Michigan, Williams is aware that he's training people who won't be working for him very long. Nevertheless, it makes him feel good when he sees one of his former employees is succeeding. "I'm happy when I see people who worked for me succeed," Williams says. He laughs. "Despite what I taught them."

IT'S WOMEN'S WORK

Let's make this clear: even though the craft beer movement today is dominated by men, brewing was and is women's work, too. In fact, throughout much of history, it was exclusively women's work. Centuries ago, brewing was a home-based activity conducted by women who were expected to raise children and bake and brew for their men who worked in the fields.

Women lost their role as brewers as the chore shifted from the home to breweries, taverns, and monasteries. By the 1700s, women were entirely excluded from breweries as "many brewers considered their presence in breweries an undesirable influence on the sensitive and mysterious process of fermentation."[9]

Gender roles and expectations have changed for the better recently, and women have proven themselves to be every bit as capable as men when it comes to designing and brewing beer. Today, women are getting back into brewing in a big away. They own craft breweries. They make beer. They work in cellar jobs. They lift bags of malt and run bottling lines.

When it comes to beer, women are men's equals in every way, so don't be misled by clichés and stereotypes about women's taste buds. Even though conventional wisdom holds that women want to drink fruity or flowery beers, women brewers insist they don't want those varieties any more or less than men do.

But women might just bring a different sensibility to brewing. If the process of making beer is both art and science, women might tend to fall a little bit more on the art side.

Take Amy Waugaman, a former brewer at the Boatyard Brewing Company in Kalamazoo. Waugaman has a science background—a bachelor's degree in biology with a minor in chemistry from Northland College in Ashland, Wisconsin—but when she's brewing she more often applies her degree in baking and pastry arts from the

"YOU CAN TELL PRETTY QUICKLY WHICH PEOPLE WILL AND WILL NOT MAKE IT. YOU HAVE TO HAVE PASSION FOR [THE] END RESULT. EVERYTHING YOU DO HERE IS TO GIVE PEOPLE THE PERFECT PINT."
-STACEY ROTH

STACEY ROTH, THE PRODUCTION MANAGER AT GRIFFIN CLAW BREWING COMPANY IN BIRMINGHAM.

Amy Waugaman, former brewer at the Boatyard in Kalamazoo. Waugaman is among the women in Michigan who are changing the face of the industry.

Institute of Culinary Education in New York City. That background in baking allows her to brew intuitively because she knows which flavors tend go well together.

That ability to mix and match inspired her to create her own original concoctions, including Lucie's Lullaby, a strawberry-rhubarb beer that is surprisingly unfruity. (There's only a slight whiff of strawberry in the aroma.) Waugaman hates fruity beer. If there's one thing she hates more than fruity beer, it's men who assume she likes fruity beer because she's a woman.

Waugaman decided to start brewing after going through a messy divorce and moving to Michigan with her three small children. On the night of her thirty-fifth birthday, she decided to try her first beer—ever. It was a Red's Rye IPA in the taproom at Founders in Grand Rapids, and it changed her life. The next day she started reading everything she could about home brewing. She watched YouTube videos. She joined a local home brewing club and started asking questions.

Waugaman's professional brewing career began when she stumbled upon the Boatyard Brewing Company on Facebook. The nascent brewery's philosophy of fostering a community fit with her own. She offered her services to the brewery's owners in exchange for lessons in how to improve her brewing skills. After just two meetings with co-owner Brian Steele, Waugaman was brewing for pay.

Waugaman is shattering stereotypes, but she still can't avoid the comments of men who think she is somehow either unqualified or unworthy. She hears negative comments all the time. The one that irks her the most is the assumption that if she was the brewer it was only because she was married to the owner.

At Rare Bird Brewpub in Traverse City, brewer Tina Schuett shrugs when asked about what it's like to be a woman in brewing. The first answer she gives is that it's fun, especially since all the brewers in town know each other. But she admits that many of the male brewers in town treat her a bit like she's their little sister. The thing that irritates her is when people come in the brewpub and automatically assume that her business partner, Nate Crane, is the brewer.

Tina Schuett, the brewer at Rare Bird in Traverse City, says she gets annoyed when visitors to the brewery automatically assume her male business partner is the brewer.

December Lee, an assistant brewer at Right Brain in Traverse City, knows how Schuett feels. Some people stumble when she tells them her vocation. "When I tell people I'm a brewer, that's when I get the most: 'What?'"

Lee worked the front of the house when she was hired at Right Brain, pouring beers and serving customers, patiently waiting for her chance to move into brewing. When she heard that Right Brain owner Russell Springsteen needed somebody back in the brewery, she raised her hand and made it clear she would wash kegs or bottle or do anything else that was necessary. Her transition to the brewery was made easier by taproom regulars who became her own personal cheerleaders. Every day when Lee clocked out, friends at the bar would ask how she did and what she did. They wanted to see her succeed.

Lee's position at Right Brain isn't unusual because she's a woman; it's atypical because she's in her forties, which makes her the oldest person working in production at that brewery. "I'm kind of like the den mother," Lee says. "Some days I feel like I'm working in a frat house. Everybody else is in their twenties."

Age issues aside, Lee doesn't believe there's any difference between her and her co-workers. She says she never gets any hassle from her co-workers—and for a good reason. "They know better."

As director of production for Griffin Claw Brewing Company in Birmingham, Stacey Roth is among the highest-ranking women in brewing in the state. Even though she has worked in brewing in one respect or another since 2002, she admits she never thought about gender in the industry until recently. In her early days at the now-defunct Michigan Brewing Company in Webberville, she says she had no problem lifting a 170-pound keg into the back of truck—or doing anything else a man could do.

Roth left brewing in 2005 when she decided to complete her college degree and get a "real job." Soon, though, she realized that she missed brewing. She missed being dirty and sweaty. She missed the community. She realized she was more interested in beer than anything else. In 2006, she applied for beer jobs and was hired after a five-minute interview with Duncan Williams at Grizzly Peak in Ann Arbor. She moved down the street to Arbor Brewing

Stacey Roth, production manager at Griffin Claw in Birmingham, at her work station in the brew house.

Company in 2007, splitting her time between Arbor and the Corner Brewery in Ypsilanti. In 2008, she moved to Battle Creek to work for Arcadia Ales.

Roth admits that, engrossed in her own career, she never considered the larger picture of women in brewing until one day a friend asked why all of a sudden it seemed there were so many women in the Michigan brewing industry. Roth realized that the industry was changing and she was no longer the exception. She met Pauline Knighton, a "beer liberator" (sales representative) for Short's Brewing Company, at a Michigan Brewers Guild meeting in early 2014 and discovered that Knighton was already working to bring women together to make collaboration brews where they could learn, grow, and bond. The two talked only briefly, but were inspired to help other women succeed in the industry.

Three months later Roth, Knighton, and other women formed Fermenta, a women-focused nonprofit trade group committed to diversity, camaraderie, networking, and education within the craft beverage—not just beer—industry. Initially Roth and Knighton thought they would become a chapter of the Pink Boots Society, a national organization of women in brewing, but with so many women working in the wine, mead, cider, and craft distillery industries in the state, they decided they would form a new organization that would include all the industries, and they would make membership open to amateur enthusiasts and students.

After only a year, Fermenta was holding regular monthly events across the state and had created a scholarship to help women attend brewing school.

Of course, attending a school that teaches brewing is a big help, but all the women brewers I spoke with had the same advice for other women who want to get into the business: be persistent. Plan to pay your dues by starting at the bottom: cellaring, bottling, cleaning, kegging. It's not fun, but such hard work proves you can handle the job as well as a man. Work smarter. Be more efficient. Learn everything you can. Study beer—its history, its ingredients, and its impact on cuisine and culture. Develop your palate. And then, when your chance comes, you will be ready to succeed.

Roth says that level of commitment is what she seeks when she is hiring at Griffin Claw. "You can tell pretty quickly which people will and will not make it. You have to have passion for [the] end result. Everything you do here is to give people the perfect pint."

BREWERY VIVANT

925 Cherry Street
Grand Rapids
616-719-1604

Breweryvivant.com

OWNERS: Jason and Kris Spaulding
BREWER: Jacob Derylo
FLAGSHIP BEERS: Farmhand, a French-style farmhouse ale; Triomphe, a classic Belgian-style ale; Big Red Coq, a hoppy Belgian-American red ale; Zaison, an imperial saison made with peppercorns and orange peel; Wizard Burial Ground, a seasonal Belgian quadruple aged in bourbon barrels

Brewery Vivant co-owners Kris and Jason Spaulding say their business is about making great beer—but not entirely.

That's a bit of a surprise coming from people who make beer for a living. It's an even bigger surprise when you consider that their brewery produces Franco-Belgian farmhouse-style ales in a city that's all about beer.

The Spauldings really bubble over with pride when they talk about the social commitment they've made to live their values through building a company with three bottom lines, equally prioritizing profits, employees, and environmentalism. Profit is the root of all good; it is what allows them to pay their employees a living wage, and it buys things like solar panels and other energy-saving technologies. In declaring that other concerns matter as much as profit, Brewery Vivant has become a leader in sustainability efforts among Michigan's brewers and is sharing its lessons with other breweries.

The brewery's sustainability efforts are led by Kris, who has a bachelor's degree from the University of Michigan's School of

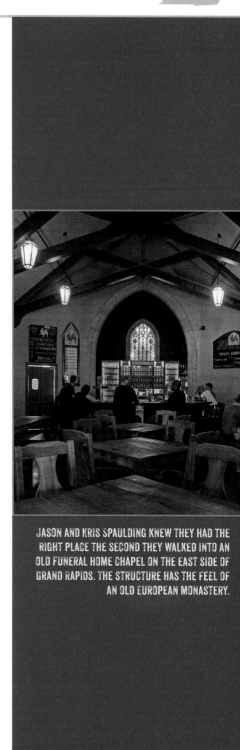

JASON AND KRIS SPAULDING KNEW THEY HAD THE RIGHT PLACE THE SECOND THEY WALKED INTO AN OLD FUNERAL HOME CHAPEL ON THE EAST SIDE OF GRAND RAPIDS. THE STRUCTURE HAS THE FEEL OF AN OLD EUROPEAN MONASTERY.

Brewery Vivant in Grand Rapids is in the chapel of a former funeral home.

Jason Spaulding.

Natural Resources and Environment and a master's in business administration from Grand Valley State University. The Spauldings earned LEED certification by designing the brewery and taproom with technologies that use less energy. (LEED stands for Leadership in Energy and Environmental Design, and the certification is awarded by the U.S. Green Building Council.) They also designed their business to earn B Corporation certification, given to companies that achieve of certain standard of environmental and social impact. The process of earning B Corp certification is both time consuming and intense, but it's helpful because it forces managers to examine ways they can improve their relationship with employees or discover new ways to work with their suppliers to help them lessen their environmental footprint. The brewery was the fourth business in Michigan to receive B Corp certification. Other well-known B Corps include Ben & Jerry's, Patagonia, and Cabot, a cooperative that makes cheese and other dairy products.

Kris's approach to assessing the brewery's environmental impact has led her to sweat the small stuff. That includes monitoring what customers are eating and what they are sending back to the kitchen after a meal. After noticing that customers who ordered burgers often did not eat the lettuce and tomato that came standard on the plate, the Spauldings prompted their wait staff to ask customers if they wanted lettuce and tomato with their burger. Why serve it if it's going to be wasted?

Instructing the staff to inquire about something as small as a leaf of lettuce may seem miniscule in the big picture, but it isn't. Little things are part of the overall effort the Spauldings have invested in their staff that has the secondary benefit of helping to build the Brewery Vivant brand.

"Everyone touching Vivant should be someone who builds your brand," Kris says. "I think we are successful because our staff is so happy. They give our customers a way better experience because they are having a better experience."

The experience is a big part of what makes Brewery Vivant successful. When Jason wrote the business plan for his own brewery after leaving New Holland as one of its co-founders, he knew he wanted to open an establishment where a sense of place and aesthetics would be as important as the beer. The Spauldings spent two years looking for the right location in Ann Arbor and Traverse City before walking into an old funeral home chapel on the east side of Grand Rapids and knowing immediately that this would be the place. "It was just so perfect," Jason says. The chapel "had this monastic feel already. And it was small and quaint. It felt like a European pub, and the other key part was it had a facility adjacent to it all on the same site."

Jason says that some customers seek out Brewery Vivant specifically because of their values. But, he cautions, a brewery cannot stay in business on values alone. That's why he and Kris also make some really great beer.

Brewery Vivant owners Jason and Kris Spaulding.

5

BEER MAKES THE WORLD GO 'ROUND

It wasn't an accident that the inaugural Great Lakes Hop and Barley Conference was held in Grand Rapids in 2015. After all, Grand Rapids proudly bears the title of Beer City USA. After tying for the honor with Asheville, North Carolina, in a national poll in 2012, it won the title outright in 2013, and again in 2016 in a poll sponsored by *USA Today*.

But Grand Rapids is also a great place to hold a conference because it's an exciting, growing community with lots to offer a visitor. There's the John Ball Zoo and Frederik Meijer Gardens, the Gerald R. Ford Presidential Museum, the Grand Rapids Art Museum and the Grand Rapids Public Museum, the annual Art Prize festival, a downtown farmers' market that's open seven days a week, and an assortment of other festivals and events.

Yet beer is no small part of what makes Grand Rapids a great town. Over the past twenty years, beer has been an economic catalyst that has transformed Grand Rapids as it has other cities, communities, and neighborhoods across Michigan.

Like many cities in the 1970s and 1980s, Grand Rapids saw its population shrink and the city's core go on life support as people fled to the suburbs and the green spaces of the exurbs. Certainly the opening of the Van Andel Arena in 1996 and DeVos Place Conference Center in 2004 spurred investment in downtown Grand Rapids, but the city lacked an identity—and hipness—until the Founders Brewing Company took off.

The brewery opened in 1997 in a former warehouse on Monroe Avenue Northwest just north of downtown. Owners Dave Engbers and Mike Stevens could have chosen a nice spot in the suburbs with lower rent and fewer problems. But they selected their location because they wanted to be a part of the culture of their hometown.

The funny thing is, they didn't just become part of the culture of Grand Rapids. They changed it completely.

> THERE'S A NEW LIBRARY GOING IN HERE, AN OUTDOOR AMPHITHEATER, A CLEAN-UP OF THE CREEK, A BOARDWALK WITH A WETLAND AREA AND A PARK. PHASE TWO IS ADDING A COMMUNITY CENTER AND A REC CENTER. . . . I THINK MAYBE [OPENING THE BREWERY] PLAYED A SMALL PART. . . . WE'RE SEEING A BUSTLING, VIBRANT LIVELY COMMUNITY AGAIN.
>
> -DAVID RINGLER, OWNER AND DIRECTOR OF HAPPINESS, CEDAR SPRINGS BREWING COMPANY

Before Founders hit its stride, Grand Rapids was known as a town with conservative values that rolled up its streets on the evenings and weekends. Now, Grand Rapids is a vibrant destination known for good beer and a thriving art community.

Michael Pecoraro of New Baltimore has seen the change, too. He's in the financial services industry and used to have an office at Division Avenue South and Fulton Street, only a half mile away from where Founders built a new brewery and taproom on Grandville Avenue Southwest. Before Founders moved to the south side of downtown Grand Rapids, there was no reason for a tourist to visit an area where homelessness, drug use, and prostitution were common. "Now they have lofts and restaurants," Pecoraro says. "Beer has a ton to do with it. That sense of community has been improved largely because of beer. I don't know if that's a fact, but I feel that."

Founders' success has spurred other brewers to invest in the city. On the north side of downtown Grand Rapids, Detroit's Atwater Brewery has moved into the first floor of an old eight-story hotel that was renovated for apartments and condos. On the west side of downtown, New Holland Brewing Company occupies the first floor of a new mixed-use residential building that takes up almost an entire city block. Slightly farther west of there, Grand Rapids' own Harmony Brewing Company has added a second location that ties into the Polish and Lithuanian flavor of its historically blue-collar neighborhood.

But although other breweries have expanded to take advantage of Grand Rapids' beer buzz, for tourists and visitors, Founders is the main draw. Walk through the parking lot at the Founders taproom and look at license plates. There are cars from all over the United States and Canada. Stroll through the brewery's taproom and you will see beer tourists tasting a flight and recording their thoughts on paper or on a smartphone app. These people probably would not have come to Grand Rapids without the presence of Founders and the Beer City designation. But here they are, also generating revenue for the city's hotels, restaurants, art galleries, nightclubs, gas stations, museums, and other breweries.

The same kind of energy is transforming communities on a much smaller scale in other parts of Michigan. A few miles north of Grand

Rapids, the opening of the Cedar Springs Brewing Company in 2015 kicked off a new round of investment in a town that had been best known for its annual festival celebrating red flannel underwear. In southeastern Michigan, Batch Brewing Company is helping to rejuvenate Corktown, the city's oldest neighborhood.

Even the State of Michigan sees the economic benefit of brewing. In August 2016, the Michigan Strategic Fund gave a $250,000 grant to Cellar Brewing Company to assist it in the move from a location on the outskirts of Sparta into a former drugstore in the heart of the city. The agency believes the move will generate nineteen jobs when the nearly $2 million renovation is complete.

The presence of a craft brewery is one of eleven indicators that a city will be successful going forward, according to the *Atlantic* magazine's national correspondent James Fallows. Fallows's list of indicators included things like the presence of a research university and effective public-private partnerships. He concludes: "One final marker, perhaps the most reliable: A city on the way back will have one or more craft breweries, and probably some small distilleries too. . . . A town that has craft breweries also has a certain kind of entrepreneur, and a critical mass of mainly young (except for me) customers. You may think I'm joking, but just try to find an exception."[10]

Bart Watson, the chief economist for the Brewers Association, the not-for-profit trade organization for craft brewers, says that even though he doesn't have any data, he does have anecdotal evidence that the presence of a brewery or breweries is a factor when people decide whether they are going to live in a certain neighborhood or location. A brewery, Watson maintains, gives the impression that a community or neighborhood is a vibrant place.

Watson says that cities with foresight are now welcoming breweries into brownfield areas that are zoned for manufacturing. A brewery provides an attraction that brings people into what may have been a depressed, neglected, or just plain forgotten area. Once a brewery brings people in, the area suddenly becomes attractive for residents, and that factor in turn brings in additional business. Suddenly a once-rundown area has become a hip and desirable one—just like the south side of downtown Grand Rapids.

Cedar Springs Brewing Company's tap-room pays homage to traditional German beer halls.

CEDAR SPRINGS BREWING COMPANY

95 North Main Street
Cedar Springs
616-696-BEER

CSBrew.com

DIRECTOR OF HAPPINESS: David Ringler
BREWER: Matt Peterson
FLAGSHIP BEERS: Küsterer Heller Weissbier, a hefeweizen; Küsterer Bohemian Pilsner, Czech-style lager; Küsterer Märzen, a Salzburg-style märzen; Blood Sweat & Tears, a pale ale

For decades, a sense of pessimism permeated Cedar Springs. While the economy of nearby Grand Rapids took on new vitality, Cedar Springs, only about twenty miles north, struggled.

The city's downtown was in desperate need of new life and vigor. There was almost no pedestrian traffic, and most storefronts were old and unattractive. Residents were looking for ways to rejuvenate their civic pride but didn't know where to start. Ideas had been floated, but nobody was willing to take a risk.

Today attitudes in Cedar Springs are changing. In November 2015, the opening of the Cedar Springs Brewing Company jolted the town out of its doldrums. The brewery constructed the first new building in the city's core since the 1950s, but it is responsible for so much more.

Since the brewery opened, the city's Downtown Development Authority has revamped the streetscape to make it more attractive. A new library—under discussion for two decades—has moved from proposal to construction. The boardwalk through the marsh in the town park, neglected and crumbling for years, was rebuilt and improved to connect with the ninety-two-mile White Pine Trail

David Ringler, owner of Cedar Springs Brewing Company, prefers a different title: Director of Happiness.

that runs just west of town. There are plans to build an outdoor amphitheater that will look like an old railroad depot, a new community and recreation center, a fountain, and a sculpture park. With all these proposals soon to materialize, talk now is turning to attracting a hotel to the area.

"People are coming out of the woodwork now and want to get involved," says David Ringler, the brewery's owner, who prefers to call himself the director of happiness. "They had been talking about doing things for fifteen years, but nothing ever happened except talk. Now something that was talked about actually happened and has been well received. People are now saying, 'Well, if that can work, maybe this can work, too.'"

Ringler established the brewery here—consciously deciding not to be a part of the thriving Grand Rapids beer scene—for multiple reasons. First, the population of Cedar Springs is growing. Located only about twenty miles north of Grand Rapids, the city is becoming a bedroom community for its larger neighbor. Second, Ringler is comfortable with the town. He lived in Plainfield Township, which is just south of Cedar Springs, as a youth and he still has family in the area. Third, he chose to be away from Grand Rapids so he could create his own identity. Finally, he wanted to create a business that would be an anchor and a destination for a small town. Ringler points to Bell's success, which has made Kalamazoo a destination for beer lovers; he hopes to do the same for Cedar Springs. Even though his brewery is not on the scale of Bell's, early indications are that it is indeed a destination. Ringler says half of his customers are from outside the area, coming from as far away as Big Rapids and Holland.

———— ⟫⟫⟫⟫⟫- ————

Ringler is a longtime beer enthusiast who started searching out unusual brands when he was a student at Kalamazoo College. After graduation, he moved to Germany and played American football professionally. During the off-season, Ringler worked for various German brewers, experience he drew upon when he returned to Michigan to work for brewers in Detroit, Webberville, and Grand Rapids.

After getting married, he decided it was time to put his degree in economics and finance to use by building an investment advisory firm. Even though he was doing boring money stuff, he kept one toe in beer, providing consulting services for importers and distributors and attending trade shows with the idea that someday he would open his own brewery. Finally, in 2013, the toe turned into an itchy foot that he could no longer ignore. He teamed up with a group that was looking to open a brewery and decided Cedar Springs was the place to do it.

The interior of Cedar Springs Brewing Company was designed to resemble a modern German beer hall.

At the corner of North Main Street and West Maple Street, Ringler and his team built a modern brewpub that would look at home in the suburbs of Munich. It features the long, community-style tables common in German beer halls. There's also a *Stammtisch*—a table reserved for regular patrons—a tradition in German beer halls.

Not only is the atmosphere warm and inviting, Ringler designed the brewery with an eye for detail. In the planning stage he worked with an architect on ways to incorporate wood and traditional colors to give the brewery warmth and make it look old and well worn. The traditional German lozenge pattern is featured throughout the brewery, but instead of using the traditional blue color that's a theme in Munich, Ringler chose red to tie in with Cedar Springs's claim to be the red flannel underwear capital of the world. The walls are ringed with flags from German cities and regions and other beer-producing countries. Even the glasses have been carefully selected to enhance the beer's presentation and aroma.

With the brewery gaining early success, Ringler says he now has two more goals: use the business to help create a stronger downtown and boost community-based nonprofits by hosting "giveback nights" to raise money for them.

ONE MORE THING: The brewery's beers are in two lines, Küsterer and Cedar Springs. The Küsterer line features traditional German beers and the Cedar Springs line contemporary American beers. If you go, you must sample the Heller Weissbier, a traditional German wheat hefeweizen. Hefeweizens have a five-hundred-year history in Germany, but this particular recipe was developed by Christian

Küsterer, a German immigrant who made beer in Grand Rapids. Even if you think you don't like hefeweizens because of the clove and banana esters, you owe it to yourself to give this one a try.

BATCH BREWING COMPANY

1400 Porter Street
Detroit
313-338-8008
Batchbrewingcompany.com

OWNERS: Stephen Roginson and Jason Williams
BREWERS: Stephen Roginson, Patrick Aherns, and Alexander Maggetti
FLAGSHIP BEERS: Batch doesn't brew with flagship beers in mind, but customers gravitate to Low End Theory, a black IPA; the Wheated, a kölsch; and the Second to Last Word, inspired by a popular Detroit cocktail invented in 1908

Some breweries start with dreams of being the next big thing. They're well capitalized and immediately start bottling and distribution.

In Detroit's Corktown neighborhood, however, Batch Brewing Company took the opposite approach, choosing to build a community of customers through a taproom—out of necessity. Scraping to find enough money to open the doors forced brewery owners Stephen Roginson and Jason Williams to take a start-small, grow-slow, do-good approach that is paying off for them and their neighborhood.

Corktown is just a stone's throw west of downtown Detroit and is the city's oldest surviving neighborhood, settled by Irish immigrants in the 1850s. For most of the twentieth century, the neighborhood was ignored and neglected. Its population shrank as many of its most elegant houses were torn down to make way for downtown expansion, businesses, and two freeways.

In 1999, the neighborhood took another blow when the Detroit Tigers closed Tiger Stadium—at the corner of Michigan and Trumbull—in favor of a modern new ballpark about a mile away. For more than one hundred years, Tiger Stadium had acted as an anchor

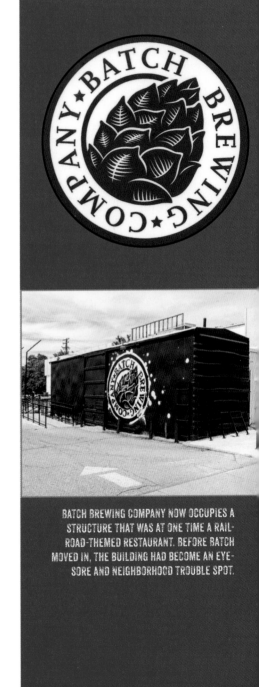

BATCH BREWING COMPANY NOW OCCUPIES A STRUCTURE THAT WAS AT ONE TIME A RAILROAD-THEMED RESTAURANT. BEFORE BATCH MOVED IN, THE BUILDING HAD BECOME AN EYESORE AND NEIGHBORHOOD TROUBLE SPOT.

Stephen Roginson, one of the owners of Batch Brewing Company. The brewery has helped to revive the fortunes of Corktown, the oldest neighborhood in Detroit.

When visiting Batch, be mindful of the house rules. The brewery's owners work hard to make sure patrons respect the people who live in the neighborhood.

for Corktown, injecting vitality and money into the neighborhood. With the ballpark gone, Corktown's future looked bleak.

But longtime residents never gave up. Many had the resources to flee to the suburbs, but they didn't. They maintained their shady streets and colorful little houses. They grew gorgeous gardens and dipped into their own pockets to support efforts to preserve the neighborhood's historic character. They also kept the spirit of Tiger Stadium alive by maintaining a baseball diamond on the grounds of the old ballpark after the grandstands were torn down—despite the disapproval of the city administration.

Today Corktown is a neighborhood that is doing it by itself. It's a place where everybody takes care of each other, which is why Roginson believes Corktown and the philosophy behind Batch Brewing match up so well.

Certainly Batch has its share of suburban visitors and beer tourists, but Roginson says he wants his primary customers to be people who can walk to the brewery. He welcomes customers from metro Detroit and elsewhere, but he expects them to be respectful of the people who live nearby. (Posted at the entrance to the brewery are the House Rules. House Rule No. 5 says: "This a family joint. Curse quietly.")

And neighborhood people are walking in. Not only is the brewpub regularly filled with local residents, the brewery has been added to the Corktown Historical Home and Garden Tour, which is held annually on the first Sunday of June. Roginson believes that his brewery was added not as a stop to slake thirsts on a hot summer afternoon, but to show people the amazing rehabilitation job done on a building that had been a longtime neighborhood eyesore. In the 1980s, the building housed Porter Street Station, a railroad-themed restaurant. But after the restaurant closed, a series of shady businesses moved in and out, including an after-hours club and a blind pig. It had become a symbol of neighborhood decline until Batch moved in.

Roginson came to the brewing business in a roundabout way. He was a home brewer but had limited time for his hobby; he had a job with a Fortune 50 company that forced him to travel more than a hundred days a year. When Roginson's job was eliminated, he started looking around for a workspace to set up his ten-gallon system with the goal of starting a nano-brewery.

Word that Roginson was trying to start a new brewery in Detroit reached Hatch Detroit, an organization that gives city residents a role in voting for the type of retail they want in their community. Hatch leaders encouraged Roginson and his business partner, Jason Williams, to enter an annual contest that grants the winner $50,000 toward opening a brick-and-mortar business. Roginson believes they were encouraged to apply because of craft beer's emerging reputation as an economic catalyst. Batch won the $50,000 grant, and Roginson doubts he would have been able to open the doors to his brewery, which he accomplished in 2015, without that boost. Now he's working to repay that investment multiple times through the brewery's Feel Good Tap.

Every month, the brewery partners with a different nonprofit. The nonprofit has a chance to spread its message to brewery customers and gets a dollar from every pint poured from the Feel Good Tap. In the first year of the program, the Feel Good tap raised nearly $30,000, including $2,800 for the Detroit Symphony Orchestra.

More than anything else, Roginson is grateful for the welcome he has received from the neighborhood and the larger community. Today, Corktown's vibe isn't about baseball; it's about food and drink. Slows Bar-B-Q moved into the area in 2005, and the neighborhood now features the Detroit Institute of Bagels, an Italian restaurant, a hip hamburger bar, a trendy coffee shop, and a number of venerable baseball bars. Roginson and other area residents are continuing to see an upswing in the neighborhood. The brewery has partnered with neighbors to refurbish and maintain a nearby city park as a place for families, not hookers and drug users. And a building that once housed an hourly hotel kitty corner from the brewery has been remodeled and reopened as a boutique.

Stephen Roginson checks a boil in his brewhouse.

"We're trying to bring something in addition," Roginson says. "What we do is authentically Detroit. It's not a version of what they do someplace else. The best way to create a vibrant city is to have things that are truly authentically Detroit. And the fact that people like our beer helps."

FORT STREET BREWERY

1660 Fort Street
Lincoln Park
313-389-9620
Fortstreetbeer.com

OWNER: Pete Romain
BREWER: Ryan Walker
FLAGSHIP BEERS: Lincoln Lager; Bedlam, a Belgian-style wheat ale; Gold Green, a Belgian IPA; Downriver Red, a German-style altbier

Pete Romain is a hardheaded businessman in a hardscrabble town.

Romain's story at the Fort Street Brewery in Lincoln Park is the opposite of the many community-renewal narratives that accompany the opening of a new neighborhood brewpub. Romain opened his brewery in 2005 in a building constructed from the ground up. In many places Romain's investment and gesture of faith in the community would have been enough to spark additional investment. Unfortunately, Romain continues to watch the area around his attractive, well-kept business deteriorate.

Lincoln Park is a working-class city with industrial roots, a bedroom community for the people who worked in steel mills and auto plants in Detroit, Ecorse, and River Rouge. As industrial America has fallen on hard times, so has Lincoln Park. The main thoroughfare that runs past the brewery, Fort Street, is dominated by shuttered storefronts, decrepit buildings, and "For Sale" signs. Romain uses his own money to keep the block tidy, hiring crews to pull weeds from sidewalks, mow the grass, and remove snow from city-owned parking lots.

But there's only so much he can do alone. Two blocks to the north of the brewery is a pawnshop, and a block to his south is a crisis

Pete Romain, owner of Fort Street Brewery in Lincoln Park.

pregnancy center. Those are not the kinds of neighbors that help to bring business to a brewery that aspires to a different clientele.

Romain has tried advertising on the radio and cable TV and in the local newspapers without much success. The most effective way to get people to walk through the door, he said, is to advertise to the state's craft beer lovers through the *Michigan Beer Guide*, published six times a year by Rex and Mary Halfpenny.

Despite its location, beer lovers do seek out the Fort Street Brewery. On a sunny Saturday afternoon, a party of twenty-five people attending a wedding at a nearby church walked in for a couple of rounds between the ceremony and the reception. The leader of the group, a man from Lansing, specifically brought his friends here because it is the only craft brewery for miles around.

Despite the lack of support from a city administration that seems to prefer gimmicks over solid economic development planning, the brewery has built up its own community—a beer fan club of sorts—and Thursday is their night. That's when the brewery traditionally opens a new cask of specialty brew. On the particular Thursday of my visit, the bar was debuting Red Devil, a traditional Irish Red brewed with Devils Claw, a root from Africa used in traditional medicine to treat arthritis and improve digestion. The root's bitter flavor gives the beer an earthy smell and taste.

Unusual brews like Red Devil allow Romain to play beer evangelist and persuade drinkers with conservative tastes to try something new. To his credit, he wins converts more often than not—and occasional visitors come back a little more often.

Still, Romain describes himself as a businessman first and a brewery owner second. He knows his clientele and location well; Fort Street Brewery has some of the cheapest prices for craft beer in the Detroit area. Romain is forced to keep prices down just to make sure people continue to come through the door. He also has regular special events and hires a band to play on the patio during Crusin' Downriver, the summer classic-car festival that attracts more than three hundred thousand car buffs. Still, he thinks he—and all the other businesses in the area—could do better if they had more support from the city. And he's not alone in that opinion.

On a quiet Monday afternoon, Bryan Craddock, the owner of

a nearby pizza joint, finishes his lunch and a conversation with Romain at the brewery. Before heading out, he too expresses his frustration at the lack of support from the city. "I thought this would be the catalyst," Craddock says, referring to the Fort Street Brewery. "The city doesn't have the foresight. People get on the city council because they have personal interest and they aren't necessarily looking out for the long-term interest of the city."

Craddock has been in business on Fort Street for more than twenty years and, like Romain, has decided to stick it out. He and Romain hold on and hope for better days, but they know there's only so much more they can take. "I'm still here after ten years," Romain says. "Ninety-nine percent of the people would have been long gone, I guarantee you."

Given what he's experienced over the past ten years and the direction the city is going, does Romain see himself surviving another ten? "I'd love to be here another ten years at least," Romain says quietly. "But I don't know."

BEER BRINGS PEOPLE TOGETHER FOR THE BETTER

For two hundred years, from the early eighteenth century to the early twentieth, the local brewery was the place for friends to meet, to talk about politics, or to catch up on the news. They were breweries, yes, but they were also unofficial community centers.

Think about how bars have fostered communities. The idea for the Boston Tea Party was hatched in Boston's Green Dragon Tavern, a watering hole for several of the fathers of the American Revolution. The labor movement may have been born on the floor of auto plants in Detroit and Flint, but taverns full of industrial workers became rich recruiting grounds for labor organizers. Surprisingly, illegal bars for wealthy patrons known as speakeasies gave women's equality a boost during Prohibition. Before Prohibition, bars and taverns were men-only establishments; women were not allowed unless they worked there—in one form or another. But not only were women allowed in speakeasies—as a way to boost profits—many women ran their own.

Brewer after brewer whom I met talked about how they wished to return to what they called the pre-Prohibition pub. Even though many of their taprooms are in modern buildings, these brewers designed their taprooms and pubs as places where people would talk with friends and strangers, not sit and watch sports on a bank of TVs. Brewery taprooms are fostering all kinds of communities. Breweries are places where friendships are born and built over beer. People come for trivia nights and concerts. They meet at brewpubs after special events like kayak or bike trips, or to travel together to visit another brewery or a major sporting event in another city.

The roles breweries can and do play in community building are endless. They can become places where communities are mobilized to support charities and schools; they can lead efforts to improve towns and neighborhoods; they can spearhead projects to build

> THIS IS NOT A PLACE OF INEBRIATION BUT A PLACE OF APPRECIATION.
>
> -LUKE DEDO, BREWER, KEWEENAW BREWING COMPANY

nature trails and pick up trash along the highway.

Your local brewpub can aid its community in more symbolic ways as well. Sometimes a brewery can be the public face of a neighborhood or actually help to define a town's identity, rejuvenating residents' pride.

And sometimes, a brewery is a place for the dearly beloved to gather . . .

ATWATER BREWERY

237 Jos. Campau
Detroit
313-877-9205

Atwater Grand Rapids
201 Michigan Street Northwest
Grand Rapids
616-649-3020

Atwater in the Park
1175 Lakepointe Street
Grosse Pointe Park
313-344-5104

Atwaterbeer.com

OWNER: Mark Rieth
BREWER: Matt Wiles
FLAGSHIP BEERS: Dirty Blonde, a wheat spiced ale; Vanilla Java Porter; Purple Gang Pilsner; Voodoo Vator, a deep black doppelbock; Atwater's Lager, a German-style helles lager; Decadent Dark Chocolate Ale

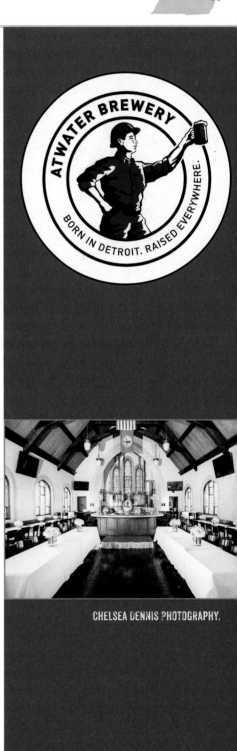

CHELSEA DENNIS PHOTOGRAPHY.

Theresa Gattari remembers her wedding as a hectic, high-stress time.

Gattari was a second-year medical student at Wayne State University in January 2016. She found time to choose the location of the wedding and buy her gown, but she left it up to her fiancé, Erick Tomaszewski, to arrange the flowers, the music, the food, and the beverages.

On Gattari's wedding day, she got up early, had her hair and makeup done, and drove to the site of the nuptials. After dressing in the basement, she came upstairs, walked around the corner into the taproom at Atwater in the Park, and immediately started to cry.

Chelsea Dennis Photography.

Pale January light streamed in through the stained glass windows. The taps, glasses, and the stainless steel brewing and fermenting vessels sparkled and reflected the light upon her husband-to-be and the rest of the wedding party standing at the end of the horseshoe-shaped bar.

It was . . . perfect.

It was only appropriate that Gattari and Tomaszewski held their wedding at a brewery regular customers refer to simply as "the church." Both the brewery and taproom are in the sanctuary of what was once Grace United Church of Christ, a nondenominational church built in 1936 and closed in 2014 for lack of congregation. The taproom's stained glass windows and high-arched ceiling certainly evoke a place of worship. Gattari and Tomaszewski live within walking distance of the brewery and are regulars at the taproom and biergarten.

Getting married in a brewery may sound like an absurd idea, but it is becoming common among craft beer enthusiasts. Breweries all across the state are increasingly acting as wedding chapels or are hosting receptions. The Detroit Beer Company regularly holds wedding receptions on the third floor of its taproom. Kuhnhenn Brewing Company has hosted a wedding in its Warren taproom, and the Arbor Brewing Company's Corner Brewery in Ypsilanti was the venue for nine weddings in its outdoor biergarten in 2015 alone. In Marquette, Andrea Pernsteiner of Ore Dock Brewing Company says it's common to see couples who met or dated at that brewery having formal wedding day photos taken of them sitting together on the swing on the brewery's second floor.

―――❀―――

Atwater in the Park is an extension of the Atwater Brewery, which is located just east of downtown Detroit. The brewery opened as the Atwater Block Brewery in 1997 in order to carry on Detroit's long tradition of brewing German beers. In fact, it wanted so much to honor that heritage that it moved into a warehouse directly across the street from the former Stroh Brewery headquarters. Despite an initial multimillion dollar investment, Atwater struggled to find its footing. In 2000, the brewery closed. Then Mark Rieth came to the rescue.

Rieth worked in the automotive business in Boston in the 1990s, where he began home brewing, starting with a knockoff of Boston Beer Company's Samuel Adams Boston Lager. He moved back home to Detroit in 1997, just as Atwater Block was opening, and immediately became a regular customer. Rieth invested in the brewery in 2002, and purchased it outright from other investors in 2005. The first couple of years were difficult for Rieth and Atwater as the Detroit economy struggled, but soon the Atwater brand began to spread and sales grew.

Initially, Rieth resisted the notion of opening a brewpub or taproom, wanting to focus on brewing and distribution. But a local investor decided it was time to revive the area of Grosse Pointe Park affectionately known as the Cabbage Patch because of the large number of young adults who live there. High on the list of ideas for new businesses in the area was a brewpub, and when Rieth saw the old church, he knew immediately it was a good opportunity.

Rieth brought in BrauKon brewing equipment from Munich and placed it on what had been the church's altar below a stained glass triptych. (Blessed be thy beer!)

The taproom was an immediate success, embraced by the neighborhood. In the summer the outdoor biergarten is full of cyclists and dog walkers, families stopping by for dinner, and late-night people enjoying a DJ's beats. During the school year, Rieth generously offers the brewery as a gathering spot for school fundraisers and other community events.

The success of Atwater in the Park has spurred Rieth to open a taproom and restaurant at the old Atwater Block Brewery's taproom on Jos. Campau Avenue in Detroit and one in an old Grand Rapids hotel that has been converted into stylish condos and apartments. In addition, Rieth expanded the brewery's capacity by teaming with Flemish Fox Brewery & Craftworks to open a brewing facility in Austin, Texas.

As of 2016, Atwater was ahead of Short's Brewing Company among Michigan-based microbrewers, distributing to twenty-four states.[11] (Bell's Brewery and Founders Brewing Company are now so large that they are no longer considered microbreweries.)

The Atwater Brewery may be getting big, but Rieth understands

Chelsea Dennis Photography.

Chelsea Dennis Photography.

how important it is to keep things local and connected to the community, which is part of the reason why two lovestruck beer enthusiasts decided to hold their wedding and reception in his brewery.

Well, that and they were somewhat desperate.

Gattari and Tomaszewski had wanted to marry in a large ceremony in northern Michigan, but pulled the plug on the planning when the estimated bill for the wedding approached $20,000.

What's more, that northern Michigan wedding just didn't feel right. All along they'd wanted a small ceremony and reception but things got out of control. The couple was so sucked in by the blandishments of the wedding industry telling them what they needed that they began to feel they were losing sight of what a wedding ceremony should be.

So in late November 2015 Gattari and Tomaszewski decided they would have a small, informal, and simple wedding in southeastern Michigan. On the Monday after Thanksgiving weekend, they started searching for venues for a January wedding—not an easy task in the time frame. That's when Gattari's mother, Anne Marie, said, "Why not Atwater?" Why not indeed? The couple had been there several times. They liked the beer, the food, and the people, so . . .

Once the plans were locked in place, the couple told friends about their plans—and were surprised by how much people liked the idea. "When we told people we were having the wedding [at Atwater], it took off like wildfire," Tomaszewski said. "People were so excited."

Based on their experience, they have no qualms recommending that others get married in a brewery. "It's surprising how great it was," Gattari says. "My expectations were high and this exceeded them."

What therefore beer hath joined together, let not man put asunder.

GREENBUSH BREWING COMPANY

5885 Sawyer Road
Sawyer
269-405-1076
Greenbushbrewing.com

OWNERS: Scott Sullivan and Justin Heckathorn
BREWER: Jake Demski
FLAGSHIP BEERS: Star Chicken Shotgun, a West Coast–style IPA; Anger, a black, dry-hopped IPA; Brother Benjamin, an imperial IPA made with local honey to balance the hop bitterness

As Michigan settlements go, Sawyer isn't even a freckle on the palm of the mitten. The tiny Berrien County town isn't a town so much as just a few buildings—a hardware store, a market, a restaurant, a pharmacy, a clothing store, and a post office—on Sawyer Road. Technically, it's really just a district for purposes of taking the census every ten years.

The area spends four-plus months a year buried under drifts of lake-effect snow and the rest of the year buried under the weight of people from Chicago who own vacation homes along Lake Michigan. But unlike touristy towns like Saugatuck and Grand Haven, Sawyer doesn't have trendy shops and galleries and fancy farm-to-table restaurants. But since 2011, Sawyer has had one thing that is both changing the face of the community and bringing people together—Greenbush Brewing Company.

Since converting an old coin laundry into a brewery, owners Scott Sullivan and Justin Heckathorn haven't been able to keep up with demand. The first year their business plan called for $300,000 in revenues; they did more than $1.5 million. To meet demand they've built an annex across the street to provide more seats and they've

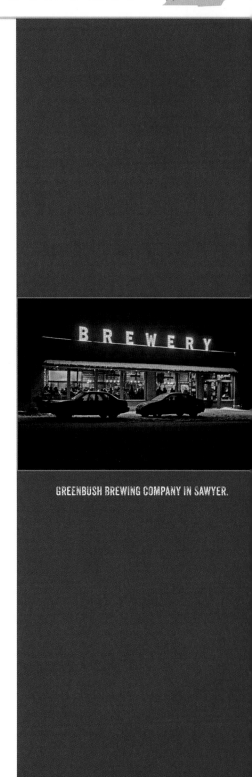

GREENBUSH BREWING COMPANY IN SAWYER.

Greenbush Mug Club regular Mark Forrest.

Scott and Kristen Campbell (*front right*) are regulars at Greenbush's Mug Club Night. Kristen has been fighting cancer for several years, and other club members raised money to send the couple to Walt Disney World for a vacation.

constructed a kitchen in an old church to cater parties, weddings, and other special events.

The success of the brewery and kitchen have Sullivan and Heckathorn thinking big thoughts that could well transform this sleepy, never-been-much-of-anything town into a destination. They plan to open a creamery, bakery, and high-end delicatessen, using Zingerman's in Ann Arbor and Dark Horse Brewing Company in Marshall as their models.

It's clear that the locals have bought in big-time. Not only has Greenbush transformed the face of the town, it has become the social center of the community, which previously had no place for people to gather.

The Sawyer census district has about eight hundred people living in it, but the brewery has more than thirty-eight hundred members in its Mug Club, including some who live as far away as Chicago and Detroit. On the weekends, locals generally stay away from Greenbush because it's packed with out-of-state visitors. Weeknights are when the locals visit Greenbush, and Mondays in particular are busy because it's Mug Club Night. Mug Club membership costs $60 and lasts for life: members get half off on twenty-ounce mugs of beer on Mondays and $2 off growlers on Wednesdays.

It was a cold, drizzly mid-February night when I was there, but the brewery was packed with people who came from miles around, including some from northern Indiana. There's a constant stream of customers, including families with children coming in for dinner. They're there for the discounted beer, but also because of the sense of community and the friendships that have developed since the brewery opened.

Among the customers at Greenbush on most Monday nights is Joseph Warburton III of Sawyer. Warburton is a jolly fellow with a great full, gray beard. He never sits at the bar; instead, he stands at one end of the restaurant against a set of brown bookshelves that are chock-full of beer memorabilia and lets people come to him.

He loves it here because of the neighborly vibe. Over the years, he's lived in California, Boston, and the Caribbean, but he's impressed by the unique affinity people have developed for Greenbush and by the new spirit and sense of hope suffusing Sawyer. "Oh, yeah, people feel the connection," Warburton says. "And by some strange coincidence, it really is good beer. . . . People come in and take pride knowing that one of the best beers in Michigan is made in their town."

Standing with Warburton is Scott Campbell, a homebuilder who lives in Bridgman. He and his wife, Kristen, are here tonight because they enjoy spending the evening with friends. He admits that before coming to Greenbush he was a Bud drinker and his circle of friends was mostly constricted to comrades in the construction industry. Since joining the Mug Club he has established new friendships that are thicker than beer and extend beyond the brewery's walls. Members of Campbell's Mug Club group often go bowling together and invite each other over for dinner.

Scott and Kristen understand and appreciate the depth of the Greenbush community more than most customers. Kristen has been battling cancer for more than a decade and knows the end is drawing near. One Mug Club Night she mentioned that a trip to Walt Disney World in Florida was on her bucket list. When Sullivan and the staff learned of Campbell's wish, they organized a fund-raiser—all the proceeds from a Mug Club Night were donated so Scott and Kristen could take a special trip together. Scott says that at first he tried to dissuade the brewery. "But they wanted to do this. They said they would pack the place, and they did." The event raised $6,000: the couple traveled first class to Orlando with everything pre-paid.

That's the kind of community Sullivan wants to foster. It's not just about the money for him. He wants Greenbush to resemble a British or Irish public house: a place people go to visit with people they know and catch up on the news. He trains his staff to listen closely to the thoughts and concerns of Mug Club members and then works to make the taproom experience better based on that feedback. "I operate off the premise that if you do it right and do it as well as you can, nobody will have a problem with that."

To say that Greenbush Brewing Company's Mug Club has been a success is an understatement. The club has more than thirty-eight hundred members, while the population of the town and surrounding area is only about eight hundred people.

ONE MORE THING: Sullivan became a brewer and brewery owner by accident. He began brewing in 2008 after a carpentry accident in which he nearly lost a finger. That accident caused him to miss work for three months and sent his family into bankruptcy.

He equates his personal struggle with changes in Michigan's economy—the decline of the automotive industry and the rise of the brewing industry. "When you're like here," Sullivan says, holding his hand a few inches above the ground, "that is where opportunity happens."

ROYAL OAK BREWERY

215 East Fourth Street
Royal Oak
248-544-1141
Royaloakbrewery.com

OWNER: Drew Ciora
BREWER: Kevin Debs
FLAGSHIP BEERS: Northern Light, a kölsch-style ale lightly hopped for a refreshing, crisp taste; Royal Oak Red, a malty and sweet red ale with good balance that won a gold medal at the Great American Beer Festival

It's a cold winter night in early February. The streets and sidewalks of Royal Oak are covered with snow and ice, and a bitter wind blows down Fourth Street.

Inside the Royal Oak Brewery, thirty or so hardcore beer aficionados are gathered in one corner of the taproom, as has been the case on the second Wednesday of every month for more than ten years. Bad weather is just a small inconvenience for this group of people, previously strangers and now friends, all brought together by beer, the thirst for knowledge, and the pleasure of trying something new.

The second Wednesday of every month is Panel, a beer education and tasting seminar hosted by Tim Selewski, the brewery's general manager and brewer emeritus. Every month Selewski sets up a program that explores a different beer style or styles from a particular region or country. Tonight's theme is appropriate for the weather: hearty winter beers.

The beer education is only part of the draw. The other part is Selewski himself, who is one of the state's longest tenured professional brewers. Selewski personifies passion for beer and has made it his calling to learn as much about it as he possibly can.

Tim Selewski, the general manager and brewer emeritus at Royal Oak Brewery, leads his monthly tasting panel in a toast.

Besides being a walking beer encyclopedia, Selewski is an insult comedian, and there is never a dull moment when he's in the room.

The first beer tonight is a dark lager from the well-respected Brooklyn Brewing Company in New York. All participants get a glass and about an ounce or two of the beer. Everyone examines the color and checks the aroma. After Selewski talks briefly about the style—calling lager a much-underappreciated beer—it's time to drink. He holds his glass up and says, "Everybody! One! Two! Three! Panel!" On the word *panel*, everybody taps their glass on the tabletop and then takes a sip. Now it's time to talk about the beer's taste and texture. Everybody agrees it's an easy-drinking, smooth beer with no bitterness.

The evening falls into a routine: pouring, discussion of style, aroma, and color, a toast, consumption, and more discussion about flavor and feel. The next beer up is Alaskan Winter Ale from the Alaskan Brewing Company in Juneau. Everybody agrees this is a surprise—but not in a good way. The label says that the beer is brewed with spruce tips, but the beer itself is syrupy and annoyingly sweet.

The Alaskan Winter Ale is followed by an Imperial Porter from Flying Dog and then a dopplebock from Augustiner-Brau, a famous brewery in Munich that was established in 1328. The beer is somewhat sweet, but not like the Alaskan Winter Ale, and has a 7.5-percent alcohol content. Selewski explains that this particular beer was historically brewed by monks with the intention of keeping them fortified during the forty days of Lent when they were not allowed to eat.*

That little tidbit about the monks sets off a discussion among participants of German breweries they've visited and which ones they look forward to going to in the future.

---

* According to the website Catholicgentleman.net, the bock and doppelbock beer styles were developed in the German town of Einbeck to sustain monks during Lent when they were fasting. "[T]hese beers were so delicious that the monks began to wonder if they were contrary to the spirit of Lenten penance. Being faithful sons of the Church, they decided to consult the pope. On the journey to Rome, however, the beer was subjected to extreme weather conditions, causing it to spoil and turn sour. When the pope tasted it, he was so appalled by the spoiled beer that he immediately deemed it an excellent Lenten penance." www.catholicgentleman.net/2015/03/liquid-bread-the-top-5-bock-beers-for-lent/.

But soon it's time to get serious again, and the next beer to taste is Cabin Fever from New Holland Brewing Company, a brown ale with roasted malt flavors. Participant Margie Suchyta of Royal Oak points out that Cabin Fever's label lists the beer's "degrees Plato," which is something rarely found on a beer produced in the United States. Another discussion breaks out; everybody in the group has heard the term, but nobody seems to know what it means—with the exception of Professor Selewski, who proceeds to explain. Degrees Plato is the scale European brewers use to measure the amount of sugar that has been dissolved in the wort. It's similar to but not the same as gravity. Selewski then offers a down and dirty way to get a rough conversion: if a beer has a specific gravity of 1.028,* take the final two numbers—twenty-eight—and divide by four to get an approximation of the beer's degrees Plato.

The group sits fascinated during the brief math lesson, but soon it's time to taste test the final beer of the night, Tres Blueberry Stout from Dark Horse Brewing Company. That beer is met with mixed opinions from participants. Some think it's pretty good but they certainly would not want more than one, while others think it pours like motor oil and tastes worse.

Aside from the beer, two things keep this crowd coming back month after month. One is the wisdom of Professor Selewski. The other is the camaraderie of the group. The members of Panel have grown into good friends. Nearly every month, some regular brings a surprise to be shared with the rest of the group. Margie Suchyta's favorite was the cupcakes made with stout and covered with frosting made with Bailey's Irish Cream. "They were *sooooo* good!"

---

* When reading gravity, ignore that decimal point. If a beer had a gravity reading of 1.028, a brewer would say that it has a gravity of "ten twenty-eight."

STORMCLOUD BREWING COMPANY

303 Main Street
Frankfort
231-352-0118

Stormcloudbrewing.com

OWNERS: Rick Schmitt, Brian Confer, and Jim Kunz
BREWER: Brian Confer
FLAGSHIP BEERS: Rainmaker, a Belgian pale ale that won a bronze medal at the 2014 Great American Beer Festival; Sirius, a Belgian dubbel; the Farthest Shore, a traditional Belgian dark strong; Fun Guv'nr, a black IPA

Rick Schmitt doesn't hesitate to say it: Frankfort is his home, and he wouldn't have opened a brewery anywhere but here.

Schmitt has a sense of both pride and ownership in this community. Besides being co-owner of Stormcloud Brewing Company, he's part owner of the Garden Theater, the town's only movie house, and has served on the town's school board and the downtown development authority.

But the pride he feels for Frankfort is compounded when he hears Stormcloud's patrons tell him how much they enjoy visiting the taproom. The brewery opened in 2013, and almost immediately he heard customers refer to Stormcloud as "our place." In fact, patrons have even given the brewery a loving nickname, referring to it as simply "The Cloud."

That sense of ownership among patrons is exactly what Schmitt and co-owner and brewer Brian Confer hoped to develop when they wrote the business plan for Stormcloud. Not for cynical or selfish reasons, either. Before opening the doors, before even brewing batch number one, Schmitt and Confer had a frank discussion of what they wanted their brewery to be. In that conversation they

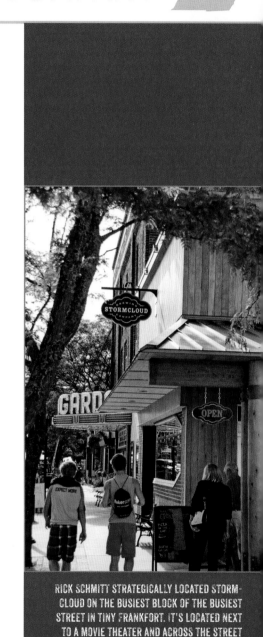

RICK SCHMITT STRATEGICALLY LOCATED STORM-CLOUD ON THE BUSIEST BLOCK OF THE BUSIEST STREET IN TINY FRANKFORT. IT'S LOCATED NEXT TO A MOVIE THEATER AND ACROSS THE STREET FROM A HARDWARE STORE TO MAXIMIZE THE NUMBER OF PATRONS.

Visitors to Stormcloud are encouraged to show where they live by placing a pin on a map of the United States.

discovered common ground; they both felt it was important that the brewery have a community-based philanthropic program. They knew from watching other small-town breweries in Michigan and elsewhere that breweries create their own communities—early customers quickly become regular patrons who develop a sense of passion for the beer, the place, and the people. Both owners thought if they could develop that sense of community at Stormcloud there could be tangible benefits for Frankfort and the region.

So as part of the brewery's business plan they created an adopt-a-charity program. Every month during the summer—the brewery's busiest season—and quarterly during the rest of the year, they invite an organization to share its message with patrons, and the brewery hosts a day where a percentage of profits are donated to the charity. In addition, Schmitt and Confer organize the brewery's patrons to volunteer their time when they seen an opportunity for a group event, like improving an area bike trail.

Since establishing the program, the brewery has teamed with local arts organizations, environmental organizations and conservation groups, a nonprofit farmstead and educational organization, and Habitat for Humanity.

The best thing about this philanthropy, Schmitt says, is he gets to see firsthand how it improves the community. "When you're running an operation that is at the center of the community—on the best block on Main Street in a destination community—you get to know other people and you realize that what you do can make a measurable and meaningful impact that you get to watch."

The taproom itself is designed to create its own community. There's only one television set and it's usually turned off. On the piano there's a stack of board games and coloring books. There's no hostess to greet patrons when they come through the door. Customers are invited to seat themselves with the unwritten goal having them sit someplace where they can start a conversation with someone they have never met before.

And then there's the brewery's other impact on the Frankfort community: because of Stormcloud, more people are coming to Frankfort for the beer. The secondary benefit is they are spending additional money with other retailers.

The brewery's business plan identified people who visit northern Michigan on wine or foodie tours as potential customers. Since opening, however, more and more transient visitors have turned out to be beer tourists working their way along Michigan's west coast. "I have no hesitation in saying that our brewery brings more people into town and elevates other business around it because of it," Schmitt says. "People travel for a destination beer experience, not unlike wine, and they are spending money in town because of us."

Stormcloud co-owner Rick Schmitt.

ONE MORE THING: Stormcloud brewer Brian Confer's reputation as one of the state's best brewers continues to grow. Of course, Confer specializes in Belgian-style beers, but his skills go beyond that style.

Confer's reputation was cemented in 2016 when the Little Traverse Inn, a gastro pub in the Leelanau Peninsula, sponsored a fun competition called the Michigan Civil Beer War. The competition was a single-round knockout blind taste test, and the beers were voted on by the pub's patrons. The quarterfinals of the competition pitted Stormcloud against the much larger and widely respected Founders Brewing Company. Stormcloud's four beers—Rainmaker, Gerald's Talking Dog, It Was A Dark & Stormcloudy Stout, and 31 Planes—not only defeated four beers from Founders—Mosaic Promise, Rubaeus, Imperial Stout, and ReDANKulus—they won in a clean sweep.

FOUNDERS BREWING COMPANY

235 Grandville Avenue Southwest
Grand Rapids
616-776-1195

Foundersbrewing.com

OWNERS: Dave Engbers and Mike Stevens
Vice president of brewery operations: Alec Mull
BREWER: Jeremy Kosmicki
FLAGSHIP BEERS: All Day IPA; Centennial IPA; Dirty Bastard, a Scotch ale that is 8.5 percent ABV; Pale Ale, made with Cascade hops; Rubaeus, a raspberry ale

The motto of Founders Brewing Company says it all: "We don't brew beer for the masses. Instead, our beers are crafted for a chosen few, a small cadre of renegades and rebels who enjoy a beer that pushes the limits of what is commonly accepted as taste. In short, we make beer for people like us."

When Founders Brewing Company was formed as John Pannell Brewing Company in 1996, there were only three "people like us": co-owners Dave Engbers and Mike Stevens and Rich Michaels, its first brewer. Twenty years later, Founders employs more than four hundred people and is still growing.

That explosive growth can partially be attributed to Founders' cultural ethos, which is to reject trends that other breweries are following. Founders was among the first breweries to brew beer with coffee, age beer in a bourbon barrel, and bottle barrel-aged beer for retail sale. Founders also created the session IPA category, which has been copied by breweries all over the country. That commitment to high-quality beer and navigating a different path has earned the brewery legions of followers.

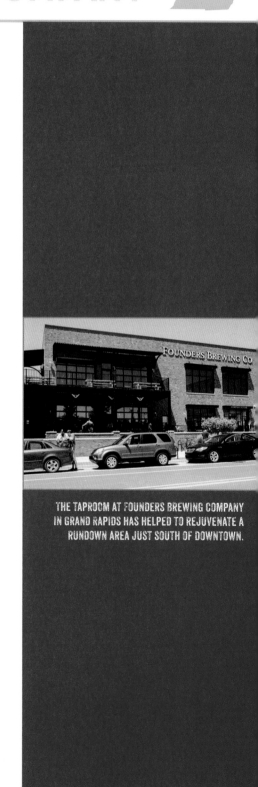

THE TAPROOM AT FOUNDERS BREWING COMPANY IN GRAND RAPIDS HAS HELPED TO REJUVENATE A RUNDOWN AREA JUST SOUTH OF DOWNTOWN.

There's no better way to characterize this iconic brewery than to let Dave Engbers, who has been called the brewery's Jiminy Cricket, tell the tale.

ON EMPLOYEES

How do we do it? We hire the best people we know. That's one of the joys. Being part of the Founders family is watching the talent of our team continue to grow and flourish.

An employee fills a keg at Founders Brewing Company's production facility in Grand Rapids.

When we started the company there were three of us. Eight years ago when we moved over here to our present location, there were sixteen of us. So, yeah, if you don't like change, Founders is not the place for you.

We've got a fantastic team made up of great individuals that share a common vision, and a whole bunch of different personalities that just work well together. However it works, it works. We are a team of individuals who share this common vision and passion for great beer.

I think one of the most important things we can do is to harness the team that we have. Listen to their opinions and get them involved and give people a sense of freedom here. It's creative freedom. Creative freedom goes a long way. I don't know how to say this because I don't want to take anything away from our managers, but typically a lot of our folks are very self-managed. We all have a goal and everyone's job is to do their best job. We set those expectations from the get-go. So people know what is expected of them. Ultimately everyone realizes that everyone is a part of Founders. Everything that everybody does affects either the liquid or the brand. And anything we can do to make the product better, that's our responsibility. It sounds simple but people do their job because they care so much about the final product.

Now, every day I see the brewery's expansion. I see new tanks, new people, new equipment. You don't take that for granted. You realize that as a growing company we continue to move forward but that doesn't mean that we don't look back and reflect. But that's the experience of Founders; we're on a straight journey.

ON BEER CITY

Mike [Stevens] and I are both born and raised here, and it was always important for us to build the brewery in downtown Grand

Rapids because we wanted to be part of the community.

I think Grand Rapids was voted Beer City USA because of the vocal beer enthusiast community that we have here. And I think that we are really good at what we do. I think that Founders played a huge role in that because we've got a great social media team on site, and that's essentially where some of the ratings have come from—it's a popularity contest and whose consumers are engaged enough to vote on these things. . . . It's whoever's community gets out there and votes.

Plus [there's] Hop Cat, a great beer bar. We've got Brewery Vivant, Grand Rapids Brewing Company, Rockford Brewing Company—a lot of other breweries that really work together on promoting our industry.

If somebody is going to make the trip to west Michigan, I hope they just don't come to Founders. I hope they go to Brewery Vivant. I hope they go to Rockford and the Mitten. That's part of the journey. You don't go to Fort Collins, Colorado, and just go to New Belgium and not go to Odell.

For our first ten years we were a struggling business. We were growing, but we weren't growing rapidly. It wasn't until 2007 or 2008—really when we moved into this location—when the city kind of took notice of Grand Rapids' craft beer industry. Some of the folks in the city administration are beer enthusiasts. And they realized when they walked through the parking lot that they were seeing people coming in from Ohio or Illinois or Wisconsin or the Carolinas. And they realized that these people coming to visit west Michigan were coming to Founders, and that's important for them because they realized this was generating revenue to hotels, restaurants, gas stations, and museums.

There's no question that the beer enthusiasts play a huge role in tourism in western Michigan. There was an economic survey done here in west Michigan that said nearly $13 million annually comes into Grand Rapids due to beer tourism.

The beer enthusiast community is vocal and opinionated but they don't mind spending money on quality.

ON CRAFT BEER ENTHUSIASTS

We incorporated in 1997. Mike and I started writing our business plan in 1994. We didn't know; we had never done this before. We thought it would just take a year to raise money and find a facility,

Fermentation vessels at Founders.

A brew kettle at Founders.

find a location. Everything takes longer than what you think it's going to.

Quite honestly, when we started the business, money never even got brought up. When Mike and I wrote the business plan, the whole idea was if we could do what we loved and make a living and live in Grand Rapids, Michigan—this is where we were both born and raised—then we succeeded.

We didn't start brewing until November of '97. So really our first beer that sold was early 1998. And, you know, we struggled the first couple of years.... There wasn't a large enough consumer base of beer enthusiasts.

We really found our path when business wasn't so great. I like to think that we, along with a lot of the other brewers that opened in the mid- to late '90s, were kind of responsible for building this community of beer enthusiasts that has really become the backbone of the category now. Beer enthusiasts tend to be very vocal and opinionated and demand better products. And that, along with the Internet—social media and blogs—all of a sudden we realized that the beer enthusiast community could go online, and that really helped build our brand. Between Beer Advocate and Rate Beer—there's a bunch of great beer websites out there—enthusiasts had an avenue to voice their opinion and be heard.

What we do for them is we hold true to our word. We are a product-driven company and it's our responsibility to deliver some of the best beer in the world. We engage with them on an ongoing basis. I spent a couple days recently in the Detroit area doing beer dinners and getting to know them. Shaking their hands, thanking them for being our customers, thanking them for supporting not just our brands but all craft beer brands. It's really important for us not to lose sight of the fact that it's these folks that helped us to get through lean years.

Here in the Midwest, it took us a little time to get on board [the craft beer movement]. One thing we realized quickly is that you can't try to duplicate what somebody else is doing, nor do we really want to. Mike and I are a couple of midwestern guys. We really embrace being from the Midwest. This is our backyard. You always try to be who you are; don't try to be something you are not.

For years people were telling us what we should be brewing and how we should run our business, and ultimately we gave everyone the finger and said we're going to do it our own way. This is who we are and this is the way we are going to do it. Since then, we seem to be doing all right.

ON BEER'S ROLE AS A SOCIAL BEVERAGE

When I was seventeen, I traveled to Europe for my first time. My parents let me drink. So when we were traveling around Belgium and the Netherlands and England, everyone drank beer and it just brought people together. During my college years, I got to travel back to Europe and again got to travel really throughout [the continent] and got to try these different beers from all these different countries. But the common thread everywhere was beer was a social beverage that brought people together.

So when we designed the taproom, immediately we said, "Everybody is welcome here." It doesn't matter. Beer doesn't care what color you are, who or if you pray to anyone, what your [IRS form] W2 looks like, who you vote for. . . . Beer is the conduit that brings all walks of life together.

I hope that as Founders continues to grow, we can be the beer that people can always trust. We hope beer enthusiasts say, "I've never had a bad beer from Founders." That's probably the highest compliment we can get. We want to build consumer confidence so that they know that whatever they get from Founders—whether it's a brown ale or an IPA—they can trust that it's going to be a great beer.

Cans ready to be filled with All Day IPA, one of Founders' flagship beers.

CHEBOYGAN BREWING COMPANY

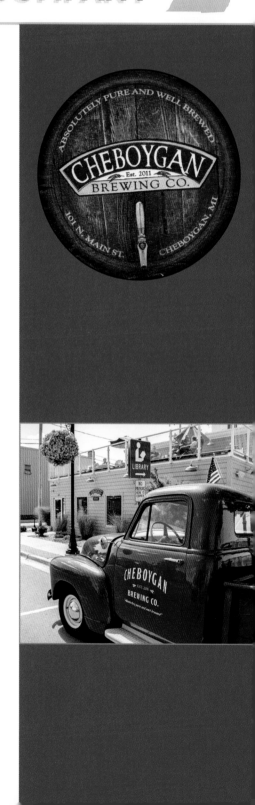

101 North Main Street
Cheboygan
231-268-3218
Cheboyganbrewing.com

PRIMARY OWNERS: Jamie McClurg and Mark Lorenz
Head of brewery operations: Mike Eme
BREWER: Brian Lindsay
FLAGSHIP BEERS: Lighthouse Amber, made with caramel malt and Noble hops; La Cerveza, a summer beer similar to Corona; Blood Orange Honey, an American wheat beer brewed with honey made from local wildflowers, blood orange zest, and blood orange puree; IPA #11, an IPA that balances malt and hops for a pleasant bitterness

When the Cheboygan Brewing Company opened its doors in 2011, there were more than a few skeptics. A craft brewery in northeastern Michigan? It would never survive in an area with a strong taste for Stroh's and Pabst Blue Ribbon.

But owners Jamie McClurg and Mark Lorenz saw an opportunity to reach into the past and restore a measure of civic pride to the city that had been missing since 1911.

In the late nineteenth century, Cheboygan and other towns across Michigan were booming as a result of the lumber industry. Cheboygan, Oscoda, Alpena, and Rogers City grew rapidly because they were important ports for shipping lumber to Detroit and Chicago to meet the needs of a swiftly expanding country. Those northeastern Michigan towns may have been small, but they had considerable pride and set out to prove they were every bit as civilized as their big-city cousins to the south. Residents built opera houses and grand government buildings, churches, and schools. But what separated Cheboygan from its northern Michigan peers and

The brewhouse at Cheboygan Brewing Company.

burnished its pride was the presence of a local brewery.

Cheboygan proudly boasted it was home to the Cheboygan Brewing and Malting Company, a purveyor of German-style lagers whose motto was "The Beer That Made Milwaukee Jealous." At its peak the brewery produced forty barrels a day and distributed beer as far away as Mackinac Island, Harbor Springs, and Alpena by horse-drawn carriage.

The county's population peaked at nearly eighteen thousand in 1910 at the height of lumber production and began to decline as the supply of trees was depleted and the lumbermen moved elsewhere. (Census records show that the county's population did not recover to that level until the 1970s.) With declining population and pressure from the Prohibition movement, the brewery shut its doors in 1911.

Cheboygan and the surrounding area struggled economically for most of the twentieth century. The town lost its passenger railroad access in the 1960s, and the Procter & Gamble plant that made paper products and employed three hundred people closed in 1990. Still, Cheboygan kept a strong sense of pride as the community became a tourist destination for boaters and summer residents.

Cheboygan may not be a burgeoning city, but it's back on the map again because of beer. Mike Eme, the head brewer, says that he's been told the number one question fielded by the local chamber of commerce is, "Can you give me directions to the brewery?"

In just a few short years, the Cheboygan Brewing Company has become an important part of the community. The brewery and taproom are in a modern new building a few blocks north of where the original brewery stood in the nineteenth century. One corner of the new brewery is given over to a display of Cheboygan's brewing heritage.

Upstairs, a second-floor deck overlooks Main Street and is a comfortable place to sit and watch classic cars and boats on the nearby Cheboygan River cruise past, people coming and going, or the town's annual Independence Day Parade. A small patio on the north side of the taproom is just the right size for an intimate concert on a gorgeous northern Michigan summer evening. It's a place for locals to gather when the snow piles up and a place for tourists and cottage owners to have a beer or pick up a growler during a weekend getaway.

Besides acknowledging Cheboygan's brewing history, McClurg, Lorenz, and Eme are conscious of the brewery's place in the community. They may not be making beer for thirsty lumberjacks, but they do make an effort to pull up a chair and chat with beer tourists and the locals who come regularly during the winter. "I'll often sit with people and chat," Eme says. "Then I'll invite them behind the glass [into the brewery]. I'll pull a glass out of the brite tank for them and watch their faces light up."

Because of that effort to connect to customers as well as the past, patrons often tell Eme and Lorenz how important the taproom has become to the community; it has filled a need for a bright, airy place where people can go just to have a beer, relax and hang out. And Lorenz says that locals tell him over and over again that they didn't realize what the community was missing when they didn't have a brewery.

Some of those thank-yous have come from people in the city's administration who appreciate the brewery's value in attracting tourists, many of whom usually head to other northern Michigan towns on the west side of I-75. "The brewery is a source of pride for Cheboygan," says Lorenz. "We can say to people that we have great recreation. Bring your boat, vacation here—and by the way, we've got a new brewery."

It may be a new place, but it has a proud history, and the past echoes through the room with every clink of a glass.

The brewery's awards on display in the taproom.

DRAGONMEAD MICROBREWERY

14600 East Eleven Mile Road
Warren
586-776-9428
Dragonmead.com

OWNERS: Earl Scherbarth, Mariann Channell, and Bill Wrobel
BREWER: Erik Harms
FLAGSHIP BEERS: Final Absolution, a Belgian trippel that won a gold medal at the 2006 World Beer Cup; Under the Kilt Wee Heavy, a Scottish export ale that contains Golding and Fuggle hops; Erik the Red, an Irish red; Sir William's Extra Special Bitter, an English ESB; also wine and mead

Loyalty.

It's tough to build it in the beer business these days because it's just not a high priority among the average craft beer enthusiast. It's certainly not like it used to be when Budweiser and Miller drinkers used to come to blows over which nearly identical beer was better. But today, with so many choices at the neighborhood market, taps at the local bar, and even different taprooms, many craft beer drinkers are too busy experimenting to develop an allegiance or affinity for any one beer or brewery.

That's what makes Dragonmead Microbrewery in Warren so different. That brewery seems to have hit on the perfect prescription. On any given evening the tiny taproom at Dragonmead is filled with a loyal customer base that has made it clear to brewery owners Earl Scherbarth, Mariann Channell, and Bill Wrobel that there is no need to advertise or run food specials to bring in more customers. "Our customers say, 'Trust us. We'll pack the place,'" says Wrobel. "And they do."

LABELS ON THE SPOOL READY TO BE GLUED TO BOTTLES OF FINAL ABSOLUTION, ONE OF DRAGONMEAD'S FLAGSHIP BEERS.

Most breweries encourage their patrons to drink responsibly. One wall at Dragonmead has a different sort of admonition.

The loyalty to Dragonmead stems from the feeling that the brewery's taproom is like a members-only club, filled with regulars who have been brought together by the beer and the companionship. Now, don't interpret this the wrong way. Newcomers are welcome—but the regulars are aware that too many could ruin a good thing.

Perhaps that's why Dragonmead looks like a brewery incognito.

It's housed in a one-story gray building on the service drive to a major suburban Detroit freeway. It's easy to drive right past, oblivious. There's nothing about the establishment that screams, *"Stop! This is a brewery!"* It's flanked on the west by a company that makes high-performance parts for racecars and on the east by a paper supply company. Many of Michigan's taprooms and brewpubs are located in unique hundred-year-old buildings or large modern facilities that sparkle. Pull into Dragonmead's parking lot and you might initially wonder why this tool-and-die shop is so popular.

But once you find it—and a parking place—entering the brewpub is an experience akin to stepping into another world. The deep brown hues, the suits of armor, mounted swords, stained glass windows, black-and-white photos, and international flags suggest an English pub, a medieval museum, or maybe a clubhouse for Dungeons and Dragons enthusiasts.

Then there's the beer. Unlike breweries that specialize in a certain style, nation, or region, Dragonmead is not particular. Brewer Erik Harms brews to style, but the beer menu features a wide selection from North America and Europe. Depending on the season, the pub features American, Belgian, English, and Scottish ales, German lagers, and even a Norwegian Christmas beer.

And yet this mishmash works. Dragonmead's small size and decor give it a scale and intimacy that is rare in brewery taprooms.

On many evenings, you can find Tom Grenke, Stuart Reed, George Allan, Pete Foeller, and Michael Pecoraro sitting together at the left end of the bar. They talk about all kinds of stuff, but topic number one every night is the thing that unites them and keeps them coming back to Dragonmead—the beer.

To a man, they all admit they are reformed Bud Light drinkers and are amazed at how much their palates have changed since their first experience at Dragonmead. At one time, they never would have considered drinking a big, flavorful beer. Now they are drawn to hop-heavy beers like Big Larry's Pale Ale or Broken Paddle IPA. "When I first started coming in, I used to only drink lagers. Who would want to drink IPAs?" says Grenke, who is from Roseville. "Now I have turned into that creature."

Allan interrupts his conversation with Foeller to comment that he'd had no experience with craft beer before his first visit to Dragonmead about six months after it opened. His first beer was Larry's Lionhart, a light-bodied English pale ale, and he has been on a beer education journey ever since.

Foeller marvels at how they have all changed. He says years ago, no one ever sat in a bar and studied the complexity of a mass-market lager. But at Dragonmead, they're interested in the flavors of the various beers and styles and spend much of their time together critiquing what they are drinking. They've become sophisticated enough to notice when Dragonmead has brewed a bad batch and when a beer—like the Russian imperial stout—is especially good.

Their loyalty to Dragonmead extends to keeping close tabs on the brewing schedule so that they will be in their respective seats at the bar on the day a new beer is released. "You want to be here that day because you don't know how long [that beer] is going to last," Foeller says.

Reed, from Grosse Pointe Woods, says he didn't know any of the guys when he came into Dragonmead for the first time. But he realized immediately that everybody had a love for beer in common, which made it easier to build relationships. Now he and the other guys share time together outside the brewery; they home brew together or drive around the state to visit other breweries. Nevertheless, Dragonmead will always be their favorite brewery because of the atmosphere and the quality of the beer.

"It's very down to earth," Reed says. "Yes, we're all beer snobs, but I've made friends with guys who have graduated from Harvard Law and mechanics, bartenders, and waiters, and we're all in the same boat. There are no class distinctions here. Everybody is welcoming. It's a good time and the beer is great. And there's always good conversation."

It's the perfect combination to keep 'em coming back.

DETROIT BEER COMPANY

1529 Broadway
Detroit
313-962-1529
Detroitbeerco.com

OWNER: Drew Ciorca
BREWER: Justin Riopelle
FLAGSHIP BEERS: Local 1529 IPA, brewed with Columbus, Falconer's Flight, and Centennial hops; Detroit Dwarf, a German alt beer; Baseball Beer, a summer seasonal

It was September 2003, and downtown Detroit was dying.

You could feel it and see it. For decades, businesses had been fleeing to the suburbs, seeking less crime and lower taxes. Storefronts were boarded up and empty, and buildings were slowly deteriorating. Grand Circus Park, which sits at the north end of downtown, was occupied by derelicts and the homeless. Even nearby Comerica Park, the two-year-old home of the Detroit Tigers, was close to empty for most of the season as the team struggled to a 43-119 record that year.

It probably wasn't a good time to start a brewery in Detroit, particularly on a block of Broadway where half the storefronts were boarded up.

Travis Fritts remembers those days all too well. He compares having a business in downtown Detroit to being in a frontier town in the Old West. There weren't gunfights in the streets, but there was a sense of lawlessness.

Fritts, who became the head brewer at Detroit Beer Company shortly after it opened, remembers Detroit police officers telling him and the other workers at the brewpub that functionally, they were on their own: don't bother calling the cops unless it's a major crime.

THE DETROIT BEER COMPANY'S LOCATION NEAR DETROIT'S MAJOR SPORTING VENUES MAKES IT EASY FOR FANS TO STOP IN BEFORE OR AFTER A GAME.

Brewer Justin Riopelle.

Certainly there were petty crimes being committed downtown, and the brewery experienced its share of them, but what galled Fritts the most were the guys who came in from the suburbs and treated the city and his brewery like they were places to cause trouble. "That bothered us because we worked there and were trying to build something," Fritts says. "For us, the perspective was, 'You don't know what you are getting into, hambone. Go back home.'"

Because of those early struggles, Fritts says, there was a lot of soul searching. Were they wasting their time? Could a brewpub like this ever work in Detroit? Could they make the Detroit Beer Company a safe place that served food on par with restaurants and brewpubs in other major cities?

And then it happened.

Fritts remembers getting to work at about 5 one morning to brew. Just as it was getting light, about 6:30, he saw a young woman walking her dog past the large windows at the front of the brewery. His first thought at this unusual sight was, "Jeez, I hope she's okay."

She was more than okay. It turns out she was the first sign of life in the rebirth of downtown Detroit in general and one block of Broadway Avenue in particular. Soon, Fritts was regularly seeing the kind of normal human activity that happens in pretty much every other major city but had been missing downtown for decades. "It was a huge sea change and it happened very quickly."

Now, downtown is livable again. Old buildings are being converted into new apartments and young professionals are moving in—including on the upper floors of the very building that houses the brewery. On summer evenings, baseball fans pour into the brewery for a sandwich and a beer before a home game. During the winter, the brewery is packed with Red Wings fans. And now, with an infusion of residents, jobs, and investment into downtown, fashionable new restaurants, shops, and galleries have moved into once-vacant storefronts and workers now inhabit once-empty spaces.

At the south end of the Detroit Beer Company's block, the Wurlitzer Building is undergoing a $20 million renovation and will soon be a posh boutique hotel. On the north end of the block, the Madison

Building is now 100 percent occupied with high-tech start-ups and an advertising agency that specializes in marketing to millennials.

The Detroit Beer Company endured through the rough times, and now business has never been better. The city's positive new vibes are reflected inside the brewery on a Thursday night. Kevin, Kareem, Stallworth, Mark, B., and Mo occupy the same spot at the bar most nights. This is *their* place. They don't own it, but they feel a sense of ownership. If there's trouble, they'll step in and politely escort the miscreant to the door. If they stay until closing time, they will help put up chairs.

They're here for three reasons: they're comfortable here, they've made lots of good friends and, of course, the beer is good.

"There's nothing negative here," says Kevin Ayers of Detroit. "It's alive, it's diverse, and I haven't met a bad person here." Ayers is a longtime Detroit Beer Company regular. He's seen downtown change since the brewery opened. Lots of hip new places have opened, especially recently, and Ayers has tried them all. He always ends up coming back to the place he calls the Beer Co.

Ayers is part of just one of the regular groups at the Beer Co. On weekday afternoons, the bar is occupied by the guys who start their workdays in the wee hours. On autumn Saturdays, the same college football fans occupy seats from one end of the bar to the other every week.

Beer Co. daytime bartender Charlie Strelecki says these regular customers mean everything to him. Some are there three times a week, some come in for Tigers games and Red Wings games, and others come in only occasionally, when they are in town for business. He gets to know each of them by name and always makes sure to welcome them back. "The community here is fabulous," Strelecki says. "That's why we've been here thirteen years and we're not going anywhere."

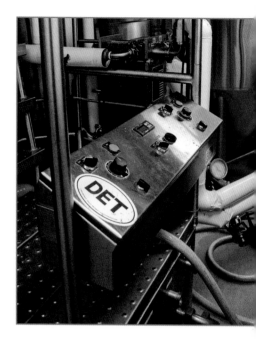

Detroit Beer Company brewer Justin Riopelle checks his gauges as he moves wort from the brew kettle to the fermenter.

FRANKENMUTH BREWERY

425 South Main Street
Frankenmuth
989-262-8300
Frankenmuthbrewery.com

OWNER: Steward Capital Management Incorporated
BREWER: Steve Buszka
FLAGSHIP BEERS: Batch 69, an American IPA that won a gold medal at the 2015 World Expo of Beer; Little Bavaria Pils, a German-style pilsner; the Hef, a German-style hefeweizen that won a silver medal at the 2014 World Expo of Beer; Christmas Town, a medium-bodied spiced ale with notes of nutmeg, ginger, cinnamon, and clove

Grand Rapids may be known as Beer City USA, but no town in Michigan is more closely associated with beer than Frankenmuth.

The small Saginaw County town that calls itself "Little Bavaria" was settled in 1845 by Lutherans who emigrated from the German province of Franconia. Legend has it that the first two structures built by the settlers were a church and a brewery. Even if it's not true, that legend should engender more civic pride than the town's current association with Christmas kitsch and greasy chicken dinners.

Besides, at the risk of stereotype, Lutherans and beer have a long history together. Even Martin Luther, the man who set the Protestant Reformation in motion, was known to be a drinker and a brewer. In fact, Luther put beer on the same level as Christianity when he said, "It is better to think of church in the ale-house than to think of the ale-house in church."

That is the tradition that runs through the veins of the Frankenmuth Brewery today. It's a modern, clean brewery and restaurant, but it is well aware that it is representing more than

Steve Buszka, Frankenmuth Brewery's head brewer.

one hundred years of local brewing tradition. "Christianity and beer built this community and we continue that," says brewery vice president Joseph Osberger. "Think about that for a second. It's not all that absurd."

Really, it's not. What is now the Frankenmuth Brewery has survived through several iterations, brushes with death, and a major tragedy. The brewery was established in 1862 by John Matthias Falliers and his cousins William Knaust and Martin Heubisch. It was then purchased by John G. Geyer in 1874 and renamed Geyer Brothers Brewing Company. That brewery was purchased out of bankruptcy in 1987 by Ferdinand (Fred) M. Schumacher and Ervin Industries Incorporated.

Beer is in Schumacher's genetic code. He is the fifth generation of a family that owns the Brauerei Ferdinand Schumacher in Dusseldorf, Germany. But instead of staying home to learn the craft, Schumacher struck out on his own when he turned twenty-one, first working at Fosters in Australia and then for Schlitz in the United States and Europe. After leaving Schlitz, he started a company in Milwaukee that imported Altenmünster beer from Germany.

On a visit to Detroit from his office in Milwaukee, he decided to drive to Frankenmuth to have a look around a town that was a hotspot for Altenmünster sales. He found a rundown Geyer Brothers Brewery that was making bad beer nobody wanted to buy and immediately saw an opportunity.

But Schumacher lacked the capital to buy the brewery outright and make the necessary improvements, so he partnered with Ervin Industries, an Ann Arbor–based manufacturing company, as an investor. Schumacher and Ervin Industries bought the brewery from bankruptcy court for $350,000 and then spent another $3 million to bring in new brewing equipment from Germany and tanks from the Stroh Brewery when it closed its Detroit facility. The new owners did one more thing: seeking to reconnect with the community, they reached back in time and rejuvenated the Frankenmuth Brewery name.

The Frankenmuth community was thrilled to have a brewer with a local focus in town again, and the city held a major celebration for the brewery's grand opening in 1988. Zehnder's of Frankenmuth, the famous restaurant that serves chicken by the busload, contributed to the celebration by baking the world's largest pretzel.

Even though the brewery was making great beer and the community was happily drinking it, trouble was brewing along with the beer. After a couple of years, the board of directors at Ervin Industries decided they did not wish to be owners of a brewery and withdrew. Schumacher found another investor, Randy Heine, in 1992 but left the brewery only two years later because the two did not see eye to eye; Heine wanted to grow quickly and take the brewery's brands international while Schumacher wanted to continue to focus on sales in Michigan, Ohio, and Indiana. Despite Schumacher's departure, the brewery thrived—making Frankenmuth brands and others on contract.

Then, on June 21, 1996, the brewery took a direct hit from a major tornado that cut a path through the town of Frankenmuth. Flying debris knocked out the warehouse doors and shattered several windows. The tornado was so powerful that it tore the building off its foundation and moved it two feet. With one wall bowed in from the winds and parts of the roof missing, the building was declared unsafe by engineers.

The owners decided to rebuild, but the brewery would come back as a brewpub. In the process, they saved one weight-bearing wall and the cellar—both dating back to 1862. Unfortunately, the rebuild took six years and once opened the brewpub struggled; the concept had not yet caught on, and the new guys faced hostility from the established restaurants in town. The brewery closed after two and a half years, then sat empty for another two and a half years before the current owners bought it out of bankruptcy in January 2009.

Today's version of the Frankenmuth Brewery is well aware of its rich history and connection with the town, and in turn the town embraces the brewery. Nearly 3 million tourists visit Frankenmuth annually; they come for a festival, to shop, or a weekend getaway. Generally, they're not hardcore beer geeks like the kind who visit Bell's, Founders, or Short's. There are more families than hipsters, and the taproom is usually dead by 11 p.m.

Even though the brewery's customer base is comprised mostly of tourists, the taproom has a fair share of local customers who come

in for the food specials and special events like the beer-pairing dinners. The brewpub also provides meeting space for community groups and regularly hosts wedding receptions and parties in a banquet room overlooking the Cass River.

In general, the beer menu reflects the tastes of the customers. Not surprisingly, American Blonde Ale—the brewery's gateway beer—is the pub's best-selling beer. It's what customers get when they ask what's on tap that's closest to a Bud Light. Even though many of its beers are brewed to the traditional German purity law, Frankenmuth Brewery has not been afraid to join the trend to IPAs and experimental beers. Among the offerings are a tangerine IPA and a blond ale brewed with jalapeño peppers.

The food menu is beer-centric, too. Among the offerings are beer cheese soup made with Little Bavaria Pilsener and a French onion soup made with Brown Hound Dunkel Lager, boneless wings doused in a sauce made with Batch 69 IPA, and a sriracha IPA barbecue sauce.

Unlike other tourist destinations in Michigan, which tend to slow down considerably during the fall and winter, Frankenmuth Brewery is busy throughout the year. One of the brewery's peak periods is the month between Thanksgiving and Christmas, when people come to shop and see the town's decorations. It's also the time of year when the brewery offers its popular Christmas Town Ale, which is brewed with cinnamon, ginger and nutmeg.

"If you're not in the holiday spirit, open a six pack and you will be," Osberger says. Amen to that.

SAUGATUCK BREWING COMPANY

2948 Blue Star Highway
Douglas
269-857-7222
Saugatuckbrewing.com

OWNERS: Stock held by multiple people
CEO: Ric Gillette
VICE PRESIDENT: Kerry O'Donohue
BREWER: Ron Conklin
Flagship beers: Neapolitan Milk Stout, a classic stout with all the flavors of Neapolitan ice cream; Oval Beach Blonde, a light ale; Backyard IPA, a session India Pale Ale with an ABV of 4.5 percent

It's a chilly, overcast early Saturday morning in late September, and fall is in the air in western Michigan. There are few tourists in the twin towns of Saugatuck and Douglas, which means there will be fewer people visiting the Saugatuck Brewing Company today, but W. Dexter Gauntlett II, head of the brew-on-premises operation at the brewery, knows that today will be fun. That's because every Saturday is fun. On Saturdays groups and individuals come in to make their own beer on the brewery's nano-system, and Gauntlett is expecting three groups from the other side of the state.

Saugatuck Brewing Company (SBC) has Michigan's only brew-on-premises operation. If you want to brew your own but lack experience or equipment or just the courage to try alone, this might be the place for you. For about $300—give or take—the brewery will provide you with ingredients and the use of its nano-system to produce five cases of twenty-two-ounce bottles. With that you also get Gauntlett's expertise, roguish charm, and comedic one-liners. You can bring your own recipe or choose one from the brewery's files. SBC will see your beer through fermentation and carbonation,

INGREDIENTS AND A RECIPE HAVE BEEN LAID OUT FOR PATRONS BREWING ON SAUGATUCK'S BREW-ON-PREMISES SYSTEM.

Joe Herrick, a brewer at Saugatuck Brewing Company, helps acclimate patrons who are using the brewery's brew-on-premises equipment. The brewery is the only one in the state that allows people to rent equipment to make their own beer.

Maciej Golebiewski's friends brought him to Saugatuck to make beer for his bachelor party. The groom-to-be is second from right.

then the brewery will keg your beer for you to package at one of its bottling stations. You can even name your beer and design and print your own labels for the bottles.

Over the course of an average year, around four hundred individuals and groups—ranging from birthday parties to restaurateurs making special one-off batches for their customers to employees sent by their companies (including Whirlpool and Pfizer) for team-building exercises—will brew on the SBC's equipment.

On this Saturday morning, the brewers show up around 9. Today's visitors are all from near Detroit: two couples from western Wayne County, four couples from Oakland County, and a group of guys from Macomb County who are brewing as part of a bachelor party. Over the next three to four hours Gauntlett will guide them all through the process of making beer. Along the way there's lots of downtime filled with beer tasting and discussions about what styles and recipes to try in the future. Gauntlett is on a mission to teach the neophyte brewers about the process and the ingredients as he educates them about Saugatuck Brewing Company in particular and the craft beer industry in general. But the brewers are having way too much fun to realize they're in class.

The guys from Macomb are friends of Maciej Golebiewski, who is getting married in about a month and a half—just enough time for the beer to ferment and be bottled for the bachelor party the night before his wedding.

When I ask what the guys were going to do with the beer—a stupid question, I know!—Conrad Bajor, Golebiewski's best man, steps up. "Ahem! Drink it," says Bajor says with a fair amount of warranted sarcasm. "The night before the wedding. *All of it.*"

Bajor explains that they came to Saugatuck because they wanted to do something special for Golebiewski and they all love beer. When Gauntlett brings out the cart holding all the ingredients and the recipe, he also has a special surprise for the groom-to-be: a tiara. Since it's all in good fun, Golebiewski immediately puts it on to howls of laughter from his buddies.

Working at another kettle are Julie and Eric Reese—both wine drinkers who, well, aren't crazy about beer. Then why are they here? Well, they've heard from friends how much fun it is to make beer, so Julie bought a brewing experience as a birthday gift for her husband. She decided to give brewing a try because they both love the chemistry and process of making wine, and seeing firsthand how beer is made might help them to understand and appreciate it more.

Julie and Eric are the kinds of customers SBC wants to reach. The more they know about craft beer, Gauntlett says, the better craft beer supporters they will be.

The small, unusual system the amateur brewers use was Saugatuck Brewing Company's original system back in 2005. But when it was replaced, SBC co-founder Barry Johnson suggested they turn it into a brew-on-premises system as a way of making extra revenue.

More than ten years on, brewery management realizes it probably would be more profitable to take out the system and replace it with additional seating for eaters and drinkers—but it's just so much fun. Brew on the system once and you understand why. And, according to SBC brewer Ron Conklin, there's a secondary benefit: when the amateur brewers walk out with their own beer, they'll usually buy some SBC beer and take that with them, too.

That, and memories of a morning when they had a lot of fun making their own beer.

ONE MORE THING: Hockey and beer go together naturally—either while watching a game or after playing in one—but Saugatuck Brewing Company recently strengthened the connection. As part of Stanley Cup tradition, every player and coach of the winning team gets to spend one day with the trophy. So when it was his turn in September 2015, Paul Goodman, the head strength and conditioning coach for the Chicago Blackhawks, brought the cup to Saugatuck. Goodman has a summer home in the region and decided to share the cup with the twin communities of Saugatuck and Douglas. As part of the celebration, Goodman used the cup to pour hops into the boil for Lord Stanley's III in VI Stout, a beer made to celebrate the Blackhawks' third championship in six years. Even an inveterate Red Wings fan will drink to that!

Julie Reese stirs the mash during an early step in the brewing process.

Patrons using Saugatuck's brew-on-premises equipment are taught every step of the brewing process and are encouraged to do everything themselves.

LAST CALL

For eighteen months, I got to travel across this state, visit breweries, and talk with some of Michigan's best brewers and people in related industries. My conclusion: we're so lucky to live here.

Michigan is in a new golden age of beer today because the state's craft beer industry was established by people who invested passion and creativity into an organic movement. They did it for the right reason. They did it because they love beer.

In fewer than thirty years, craft brewing has gone from a grassroots movement of people who love beer to a mature industry. The pioneer brewers have recently been joined by others whose motivations are less pure. And now with so many breweries in the state, there are signs that trouble is brewing.

First, there are indications that craft beer could be reaching the limits of its growth. There soon may be so many Michigan breweries producing so much beer that the market could become saturated. Brewers are already expressing concern that the fight over shelf space in grocery stories and markets will get intense. But the bigger fear is that competition will lead brewers to prioritize profit margin over quality, which will lead them to cheapen their product in order to compete.

That prospect really concerns Bill Wamby, a former brewer at Redwood Steakhouse and Brewery in Flint who is now a consultant to the beer industry. Wamby, one of the state's most honored brewers, senses that some Michigan brewers don't feel they need to make great beer because they can make an adequate profit with merely good beer.

At one time, Wamby says, brewers had to make beers that were outstanding for two reasons. First, the beer had to be great to lure drinkers away from the mainstream. Second, the beer had to be great to satisfy their own standards. Now, Wamby believes, newer brewers are allowing those standards to slip because they don't *need* to make great beer for profit and they don't require it of themselves, either.

Every brewer, Wamby says, should be striving to be better every day. Every brewer should live, breathe, eat, and sleep beer because the level of commitment is reflected in the product.

The second concern for the future of Michigan beer is succession. What happens when Michigan's brewing pioneers decide it's time to retire? You might wonder what harm could result when a longtime, respected owner sells the brewery and retires to a place with good beer, more sunshine than Michigan, and maybe another challenge. The fear is that a brewery will lose its identity, values, creativity, and cachet by selling to another company, particularly if it's a global brewing conglomerate. Larry Bell has already taken steps to make sure his brewery stays in the family, but what happens to Short's when Joe and Leah decide they've had enough? Do they sell out or issue stock and become anonymous corporations themselves? What would Short's be without Joe's personality there to guide it and represent it to the public?

Finally, with so many breweries opening, longtime brewers are sensing that the tight bond among Michigan brewers is starting to fray. That bond, brewers say, helped to drive their continual improvement and inspired them to be better in a collegial attempt to outdo one another.

"I pride myself on knowing what's going on in the craft beer world. I used to be able to know every head brewer by name, all the brewery owners by name," says Jason Spaulding of Brewery Vivant in Grand Rapids. "I've given up now. I can't keep track. I don't know where the market is going anymore. It's beyond what I can comprehend."

Travis Fritts, brewer at Old Nation Brewing Company in Williamston, agrees that things are changing. "What beer was back then was a community of disciplined people. You had to do it because you couldn't do anything else because you got that bug. There's still passion and soul, but it's not the kind that it was back in the day."

Nevertheless, passion for Michigan beer continues to grow among consumers, but it's generally expressed passively through the choices we make in taprooms and stores. But we consumers, imbibers, enthusiasts, geeks, and connoisseurs should be more active in our passion. We should adopt the philosophy of the state's most ardent brewers and dedicate ourselves to improving our beer knowledge. Brewers in general love their customers, but they are also quietly disdainful of the guy who drinks nothing but IPAs and thinks he's superior to the guy who drinks only pilsners.

There's an entire spectrum of beers being made in Michigan, and brewers want their customers to grow by trying new beers and different styles. If brewers could, they would encourage that IPA snob to explore the range of IPAs from several different breweries to discover how different recipes and hops impact flavor. If they could, they would encourage drinkers to change their choices with the seasons. Summer is a great time to experiment with pilsners, German helles and hefeweizens, Belgian wits, saisons, sours, and beers flavored with blueberries or peaches. Fall is a good time for stouts and porters, ambers, märzens, dunkles, and beers made from freshly harvested, unprocessed hops. Winter, of course, offers spiced Christmas beers, but it also offers winter whites and strong ales. Spring is a great time to try bocks and dopplebocks—the Lenten beers often referred to as liquid bread. Take notes on paper or on your smartphone app if you must, but don't ever become so serious that you forget to have fun.

The challenge to learn and grow should lead you to a higher appreciation for beer in general. You may not care for the blandness of an American-style pilsner, but you have to respect Budweiser and Miller for their consistent quality.

⇻⇉⇉⇉⇻

Of course, as was demonstrated in Peter Blum's book *Brewed in Detroit*, nothing lasts forever. Brewing is an industry that is constantly in flux because tastes change over time. Besides, any organic movement that is perceived as new, different, and hip is eventually co-opted and dragged into the mainstream. That's where we are with craft beer today.

But craft beer is also in a healthy place because the seeds have been sown for the future. There may currently be people in Michigan jumping into the industry for the wrong reasons, but the first generation of craft brewers—the people who founded and built the industry because they couldn't imagine doing anything else with their lives—has set the standard. And sitting in a Michigan taproom somewhere today are young people who are going to be the next Ben Edwards, Ted Badgerow, Larry Bell, Eric and Bret Kuhnhenn, Bill Wamby, or Stacey Roth.

I look forward to visiting their taprooms soon. Cheers!

NOTES

1 "Craft Brewing Industry Boosts Michigan Economy by $1.85 Billion, New Report Finds," *MiBiz*, accessed July 1, 2016, mibiz. com/news/food-biz/item/23103-craft-brewing-industry-boosts-michigan-economy-by-?tmpl=component.

2 Amy Sherman, "Michigan Brewers Are at the Top of Their Game, Even Jim Koch Thinks So," MLive.com, accessed January 12, 2017, www.mlive.com/beer/2017/01/michigan_brewers_are_at_the_to.html#19.

3 Ashley McFarland, Christian Kapp, Russell Freed, Jim Isleib, and Scott Graham, "Malting Barley Production in Michigan," *Michigan State University Extension Bulletin* GMI-035, July 2014.

4 Thomas H. Walters, "Michigan's New Brewpub License: Regulation of Zymurgy for the Twenty-First Century," *University of Detroit Mercy Law Review* 71 (1994), 621.

5 David Bardallis, *Ann Arbor Beer: A Hoppy History of Tree Town Brewing* (Charleston, SC: History Press, 2013), 124.

6 Eric Asimov, "A Delicious Free-for-All," *New York Times*, February 24, 2010.

7 "How Metro Detroit Became a National Leader in Mead Making," *Second Wave Homepage,* March 5, 2015, accessed December 22, 2015, www.secondwavemedia.com/metromode/features/metrodetroitmead030515.aspx?fb_comment_id=702553846532877_702782173176711#f9f30dd2.

8 "Schramm's Mead: Ferndale, Michigan," accessed December 22, 2015, www.ratebeer.com/p/schramms-mead/39305/.

9 Peter H. Blum, *Brewed in Detroit: Breweries and Beer since 1830* (Detroit: Wayne State University Press, 1999), 28.

10 James Fallows, "Eleven Signs a City Will Succeed," *Atlantic*, March 2016.

11 Robert Allen, "How Top Michigan Craft Brewers Aim to Take Over the Country," *Detroit Free Press*, January 3, 2017, www.freep.com/story/entertainment/2017/01/02/michigan-beer-breweries-growth/93951458/.

INDEX

AB InBev, 15, 39

ABC India, 45, 46–49

Acoustic Draft Mead, 78

Alaskan Brewing Company, 172

Allen, George, 190–91

Arktos Meadery, 78

American Homebrewers Association, 77, 78

Anchor Brewing Company, 34

Anheuser-Busch Brewery, 11, 15, 27

Ann Arbor Beer: A Hoppy History of Tree Town Brewing, 47

Ann Arbor, Michigan, 12, 32, 35, 36, 66, 69, 101; and Arbor Brewing, 45–49, and Grizzly Peak, 16, 25, 31, 47, 72, 120, 131, 137

Arbor Brewing Company, 12, 31, 45–50, 120, 131, 137–38, 164

Arcadia Brewing Company (Arcadia Ales), 31, 131, 138

Archiable, Jack, 11, 25, 65

Atlantic, 147

Atwater Brewery, 27, 31, 119, 146, 163–66

Atwater in the Park, 4, 163–66

Averill, Gordon, 34–35

Axle Brewing Company, 115

Ayers, Kevin, 195

B. Nektar, 45, 76

Bad Brewing, 83

Bad Frog Beer, 32

Badgerow, Ted, 34–36, 208

Bajor, Conrad, 202

Banks, Wendell, 14

Bardallis, David, 47

Barley, 12

Barrett, John, 95–97

Batch Brewing Company, 26, 119, 147, 153–55

Battle Creek, Michigan, 31, 131, 138

Bear River Brewing, 32

Beer Advocate, 182

Beer City USA, 145, 146, 180–81, 197

Beggars Brewery, 67

Bell, David, 39

Bell, Larry, 2, 3, 28, 30, 31, 33, 35, 37–39, 41, 206, 208

Bell, Laura, 39

Bellaire, Michigan, 4, 55, 57, 60, 62

Bell's Brewery, 3, 16, 28, 37–39, 150, 165, 199

Bengaluru, India, 46–49

Beratta, Adam, 115

Big Buck, 32, 114

Bitter Old Fecker Rustic Ales, 132

Blue Tractor, 132

Blum, Peter, 6, 207

Blackrocks Brewery, 9

Blind Tiger Brewery and Restaurant, 32

Boatyard Brewing Company, 135–36

Bo's Brewery and Bistro, 32

Borsius, Ed, 101–3

Boston Beer Company, 165

Boulder Brewing Company, 30

Brauerei Ferdinand Schumacher, 198

Breimayer, Chris, 81–83

Breimayer, Pat, 81–83

Brettanomyces, 70

Brew Detroit, 11, 26

Brewbakers Craft Brewery and Bakehouse, 32

Brewed in Detroit, 6, 207

Brewers Association, 4, 27, 130, 147

Brewery Terra Firma, 67

Brewery Vivant, 141–43

Brewing process, 11–24; carbonation, 24–25; diacetyl, 23–24; DMS, 19; dry hopping, 23; fermentation, 12, 13, 17, 19, 20–25, 59, 70, 71, 135; pasteurization, 26; yeast, 12, 13, 14, 17, 20–23, 24, 26, 38, 63, 70–71, 74, 76, 117

Brickskeller Dining House and Down Home Saloon, 38

Brite Eyes Brewing Company, 91–93

Brower, Michael, 88–89

Burns, Priscilla, 30

Burns, Thomas, Jr., 30, 32, 33, 42

Buszka, Steve, 33, 197, 198

Campbell, Kristen, 169

Campbell, Scott, 169

Cantillon (beer), 72

Carlson, Jon, 73, 131

Cartright Brewing Company, 30

Cedar Springs Brewing Company, 145, 147, 149–51

Cedar Springs, Michigan, 149–51

Cellar Brewing Company, 147

Central Michigan University, 13, 107

Channell, Mariann, 189

Cheboygan Brewing Company, 117, 185–87

Cheboygan, Michigan, 195–87

Chelsea, Michigan, 33, 34, 35, 132

CJ's Brewing Company, 42

Complete Joy of Home Brewing, 78

Compleat Meadmaker, 76

Confer, Brian, 175

Conklin, Ron, 203

Connor, Konrad, 113–15

Coors Brewing Company, 11, 15, 27

Copper Canyon Brewery, 32

Corner Brewery, 12, 138, 164

Craddock, Bryan, 158–59

Craft Cultures, 21

Craftwerk Brewing Systems, 81

Crane, Nate, 136

Dark Horse Brewing Company, 23, 32, 45, 117, 123–25, 168, 173

Dedo, Luke, 161

Degrees Plato, 173

DeMattei, Cordell, 13

Demski, Jake, 167

Derylo, Jacob, 141

Detroit, Michigan, 2, 18, 26, 29, 31, 33, 41, 43, 73, 76, 119, 146, 150, 153–55, 157, 161, 164, 165, 168, 185, 190, 190, 193–95, 198

Detroit & Mackinac Brewing Company, 32–33, 42

Detroit Beer Company, 193–95

Dexter, Michigan, 4, 12, 69, 70, 72, 73, 132

Diacetyl, 24

Dimethyl sulfide (DMS), 19

Doane, Chad, 88

Dragonmead Microbrewery, 11, 32, 119, 126, 189–91

Duster's Microbrewery, 32

Duvel Moortgat, 39

Eccentric Café, 37

Edwards, Ben, 2–3, 29–30, 32, 33, 208

Eme, Mike, 117, 185–87

Elk Rapids, Michigan, 3, 32, 55, 59, 62

Elk Street Brewery and Taproom, 105–8

Elysian Brewing Company, 39

Empire Hops Farm, 18

Ervin Industries, 198–99

Engbers, Dave, 27, 118, 145, 179–83

Falliers, John Matthias, 198
Fallows, James, 147
Fermenta, 138
Ferndale, Michigan, 75, 76, 106, 115
Filling Station Microbrewery, 21
Fire Academy Brewery and Grill, 32
Firestone-Walker Brewing Company, 39
Flemish Fox Brewery & Craftworks, 165
Flint, Michigan, 8, 113, 115, 161, 205
Flying Dog Brewery, 172
Foeller, Pete, 190–91
Fort Street Brewery, 157–59
Founders Brewing Company, 3, 16, 32, 118, 136, 145, 146, 165, 177, 199; and Mahou San Miguel, 27, 45;
Franco-Belgian–style beer, 4, 69, 70, 141
Frankenmuth Brewery, 30, 33, 197–200
Frankfort, Michigan, 175–78
Fritts, Travis, 193–94, 206
Frog Island Brewing Company, 32,

G. Heileman Brewing Company, 30
Galovan, Angie, 100
Gattari, Anne Marie, 166
Gattari, Theresa, 163–66
Gauntlett II, Dexter, 201–3
Geiger, Emily, 21–23
Geyer Brothers Brewing Company, 198
Geyer, John, G. 198
Golebiewski, Maciej, 202
Good Harbor Ale, 73
Goodman, Paul, 203
Grace, Brian, 132
Grand Rapids, Michigan, 32, 33, 78, 118, 136, 141–43, 145–46, 147, 150, 152; and

Atwater Brewery, 146, 163, 165; and Brewery Vivant, 141–43, 206; and Founders Brewing Company, 179–83
Grand Rapids Brewing Company, 31, 181
Great American Beer Festival, 4, 51, 55, 62, 63, 73, 113–14, 171, 175
Greenbush Brewing Company, 119, 167–70
Greenville, Michigan, 81, 82
Greff, Matt, 12, 31, 45–50
Greff, Rene, 31, 45–50
Grenke, Tom, 190–91
Griffin Claw Brewing Company, 2, 131, 133, 135, 137, 139
Grizzly Peak Brewing Company, 16, 25, 31, 47, 70, 72, 120, 131–33, 137
GW Kent, 81

Halfpenny, Mary, 158
Halfpenny, Rex, 32, 118–19, 158
Hansen, Tony, 58
Harmony Brewing Company, 146
Harms, Erik, 189, 190
Hasenbusch, Anne and Ron, 105–8
Hatch Detroit, 155
Heckathorn, Justin, 167–68
Heine, Randy, 199
Heineken NV, 39
Hereford and Hops Steakhouse and Brewpub, 31
Hertel, Curtis, Sr., 30–31
Heubisch, Martin, 198
Hong Kong International Beer Awards, 73
Hops, 11, 12, 13, 16–19; dry hopping, 23; hop farming, 5, 49, 105, 107
Houghton, Michigan, 21
Hukill, Nathan, 132

International Bitterness Units (IBUs), 17–18, 108

Jeffries, Laurie, 72, 73
Jeffries, Ron, 4, 12, 51, 69–74, 132
John Pannell Brewing Company, 32
Johnson, Barry, 203
Jolly Pumpkin Artisan Ales, 4, 12, 43, 45, 51, 69–74, 132

Kalamazoo Brewing Company, 30, 31, 37
Kamp, Joel, 88
Keweenaw Brewing Company, 21, 161
King Brewing Company, 128
Knaust, William, 198
Knighton, Pauline, 138
Knudson, Bill, 15
Koch, Jim, 7
Kuhnhenn, Bret, 119, 127–30, 208
Kuhnhenn Brewing Company, 27, 45, 76, 119, 127–30, 164
Kuhnhenn, Eric, 119, 127–30, 208
Kuhnhenn, Eric, Sr., 127–28
Küsterer, Christian, 151–52

Lagunitas Brewing Company, 39
Largent, Andy, 21
LeClaire, Adam, 53
Lee, December, 137
Linardos, John, 32, 33, 41–43, 120
Lincoln Park, Michigan, 157–59
Little Traverse Inn, 177
Lobdell, Greg, 131
Local Color Brewing Company, 32
Lorenz, Mark, 185–87
Ludlow, Barrett, 96
Ludlow, Lark, 95–98

Luther, Martin, 197

Mackinac Brewing Company, 32
Mahou San Miguel, 27, 45
Malt, 13, 14, 16, 17, 20, 26, 51, 61, 70, 71, 78, 91, 109; malting process, 13–14
Marquette, Michigan, 9, 109–10, 164
Maytag, Fritz, 34
McAuliffe, Jack, 33
McCabe, Susan, 18
McClurg, Jamie, 185, 187
Mead, 12, 75–79, 93, 138, 189
Michaels, Rich, 179
Michigan Beer and Wine Wholesalers Association, 31
Michigan Beer Guide, 32, 118, 158
Michigan Brewing Company, 32, 137
Michigan Brewers Guild, 7, 23, 119, 138
Michigan Liquor Control Commission, 29–30, 31
Michigan Malt, 14
Michigan Mobile Canning Company, 26,
Michigan State University Extension Service, 15
Michigan Strategic Fund, 147
Michigan Technological University, 22
Miller Brewing Company, 11, 27, 189, 207
Mishigama Brewing Company, 36
Morse, Aaron, 117, 123–25
Morse, Kristine, 125
Motor City Brewing Works, 32, 41–43, 119, 120
Mitten Brewing Company, 181

New Albion Brewing Company, 33
New Belgium Brewing Company, 181
New Holland Brewing Company, 12, 31, 143,

146, 173

New York Times, 73

North Peak Brewing Company, 70, 132

Northern Michigan University, 110–11, 125

Northern United Brewing Company, 69, 70, 132

Odell Brewing Company, 181

Old Mill Brewpub & Grill, 99–100

Ore Dock Brewing Company, 109–11

Osberger, Joseph, 198, 200

Paddle Hard Brewing Company, 85

Panchamé, Nick, 64, 65–66

Papazian, Charlie, 78

Parker's Hilltop Brewery, 115

Pecoraro, Michael, 146, 190

Pernsteiner, Andrea, 109–11

Pernsteiner, Weston, 109–11

Perrin Brewing Company, 52–53

Peterson, Matt, 149

Pfeiffer, Bill, 78

Pierce, Brian, 91–93

Pierce, Shelby, 91–93

Pigeon Hill Brewing Company, 87–89

Plainwell, Michigan, 99–100

Psycho Brew, 81–83

Rare Bird Brewpub, 67, 136

Ratebeer.com, 76, 77, 182

Real Ale Company, 34–36

Redwood Steakhouse and Brewery, 113–15

Reed, Stuart, 190, 91

Reese, Eric and Julie, 202–3

Ribbon Hops Farm, 18

Rieth, Mark, 119, 163, 164–65

Right Brain Brewery, 19, 28, 51, 52, 63–67,

117, 121, 136–37

Ringler, David, 145, 149–51

Riopelle, Justin, 193, 194, 195

Roberts, David, 36

Rockford Brewing Company, 181

Roginson, Stephen, 26, 119, 153–55

Romain, Pete, 157–59

Roth, Stacey, 131, 133, 135, 137–39, 208

Royal Oak Brewery, 171–73

St. Ambrose Meadery, 78

Salt Springs Brewery, 101–3

Sandusky, Michigan, 105–8

Saugatuck Brewing Company, 24, 201–3

Saugatuck, Michigan, 167, 202, 203

Sawyer, Michigan, 167–70

Scarsella, Daniel, 41–43, 132

Scherbarth, Earl, 189

Schmidt, Tim, 131

Schmitt, Rick, 175–77

Schofield, Ron, 101–3

Schramm, Ken, 75–79

Schramm's Mead, 75–79

Schuett, Tina, 136

Schumacher, Ferdinand M., 198–99

Seifer, Barry, 31

Selewski, Tim, 171–73

Shaw, David, 115

Shelton Brothers Importing, 72–73

Shelton, Dan, 73

Shelton, Joel, 72

Shepherd, Michigan, 14, 37

Sherwood, Sam, 63, 66

Short, Joe, 55–62, 65, 206

Short, Leah, 55–62, 206

Short's Brewing Company, 3, 4, 13, 25, 45, 52, 55–62, 63, 138, 165, 206; Bellaire Pub, 55

Sikka, Gaurav, 48–49
Sparta, Michigan, 147
Spaulding, Jason and Kris, 141–43
Springsteen, Russell, 19, 63–67, 117, 121, 137
Steele, Brian, 135
Stevens, Mike, 145, 179, 180
Stewart, John, 53
Stormcloud Brewing Company, 175–77
Strelecki, Charlie, 195
Stroh Brewery, 2, 3, 5, 6, 11, 12, 14, 17, 23, 26, 30, 164, 198
Suchyta, Margie, 173
Sullivan, Scott, 119, 167–70

Tahquamenon Falls Brewery & Pub, 95–97
Tecumseh Brewing Company, 132
Tenacity Brewing Company, 8
Time, 35
Tomaszewski, Erick, 163–66
Traffic Jam and Snug, 29, 30, 31, 32
Traverse Brewing Company, 32, 65
Traverse City, Michigan, 15, 18, 21, 32, 69, 78, 83, 106, 132, 136; and Right Brain Brewery, 19, 28, 51, 52, 63–67, 117, 121, 136–37

Unita Brewing Company, 39

Vander Mill LLC, 78
Vanilla Java Porter, 26, 27
Vancourt, Nick, 109, 111
Vargo, Dave, 85
Wamby, Bill, 29, 114–15, 205–6, 208
Warburton, Joseph, III, 168
Watson, Bart, 147
Waugaman, Amy, 135–36
Wayne State University Press, 6
Wiesen, Alex, 18

Wiesen, Dan, 18
Williams, Duncan, 16, 120, 131–32, 133, 137
Williams, Jason, 119, 153, 155
Wiltse, Dean, 31
Wolverine State Brewing Company, 132
Workshop Brewing Company, 65, 67
World Beer Cup, 129
Wrobel, Bill, 119, 189

Yeast, 1, 11; Belgian yeast, 70, 127; German ale yeast, 131; wild yeast, 70–71, 75
Ypsilanti Ale House, 36

Zadvinskis, Mark, 102–3
Zylstra, Scott, 99–100
Zymurgy, 77